EVERYDAY
KNITTING

the complete beginner's guide

Megan Goodacre

Publisher Mike Sanders
Art & Design Director William Thomas
Editorial Director Ann Barton
Editor Christopher Stolle
Compositor Ayanna Lacey
Photographer Megan Goodacre
Proofreader Jean Bissell
Indexer Carol Roberts

First American Edition, 2024
Published in the United States by DK Publishing
1745 Broadway, 20th Floor, New York, NY 10019

The authorized representative in the EEA is Dorling Kindersley
Verlag GmbH. Arnulfstr. 124, 80636 Munich, Germany

A catalog record for this book
is available from the Library of Congress.
ISBN 978-0-7440-9254-7

DK books are available at special discounts when purchased
in bulk for sales promotions, premiums, fund-raising, or
educational use. For details, contact SpecialSales@dk.com

Printed and bound in China

www.dk.com

Contents

Introduction

Have you ever wondered, "Why knit?"

Crafting the simplest thing is fulfilling, whether it's a birthday card, a flower arrangement, or a fresh loaf of bread. Knitting is no different. The pleasure of transforming yarn into something new is deeply satisfying. And for many people, knitting is more than satisfying, it's also therapeutic. The quiet repetition of putting one stitch after another is soothing and makes time pass easily.

Knitting connects you with others. Start knitting, and you become part of something big. There's a big group of knitting friends waiting for you; they're at your local yarn store, knitting group, and online. You'll get to share, learn, and receive praise for your handiwork. And with the techniques you'll learn in this book, you'll get to teach other new knitters!

How to Use This Book

You don't need any knitting experience to use this book. You'll start by learning some basics, step by step. There are lots of photographs and tips to help. When you start, you might want to use the book like a guided tour: don't wander off the path too much—at least in Part 1. Then, when you're comfortable with the basics, feel free to pick the techniques and patterns that excite you the most.

The knitting patterns use the skills and techniques you'll learn in this book. At the beginning of each pattern, I list the skills needed to complete it. I also gave each pattern a difficulty rating, from 1 to 5, with 1 being the easiest and 5 being the most advanced.

I'm so happy you're joining me on this knitting journey! With this book, you'll unravel (no pun intended) the mysteries of getting the stitches onto your needles and in the right place. You'll start by casting on your first stitch and end by knitting scarves, hats, and even a sweater or two.

Oh, and don't forget to have fun!

For knitters, future, past, and present.
And with love to my three Cs.

Acknowledgments

All the yarn shown in this book was generously provided by Knit Picks.

This book was so much fun to write and photograph, even when I was holding the shutter-release in my teeth, casting on with one hand, and making lunches with the other. But this was definitely a group effort, and I have to say thank you to many people: the editors and designers at DK, who brought everything together and made it beautiful. Marilyn Allen, of Allen O'Shea Agency, for playing matchmaker. Stacey Winklepleck at Knit Picks, for her continued support. My family, for tolerating my monopolizing all horizontal (and some vertical) surfaces with camera and yarn paraphernalia. My mom, who taught me how to knit in the first place. Teresa Goble, for being my knitting club, even if knitting was usually lunch. Finally, the knitters: Jan Malone, who made many of the samples you see in this book. Plus the wonderful testers who found my typos and knit like the wind: Amanda Gil, Amy Fraasch-Vold, Amy Machael, Ann Bradley, Ann Campbell, Ann Mikeal, Aurelia Criffo', Barbara MacIntosh, Carolyn S. Willoughby, Cheri McEwen, Christine Babron, Cornelia Spoor, Crystal Edmoundson, Deborah Shackford, Debra Nelsen, Donna Brisbois, Dora Lenchuk, George Roberts, Heidi Stagner, Isabel Nasi, Jaishree Venu, Jana Pihota, Jennifer Floyd, Jodi Marie Harper, Jody Strine, Josephine Colmenares, Karen Hogg, Karen Lier, Kim Lian Ng, Kimberly Conover, Laure Kwon, Linda Randall, Lori Veteto, Lynda Magsaysay, Lynn Hensley, Margaret Walton, Meg Walker, Melanie Lepage-Forest, Melissa Turner, Natalia Ingham, olive2, Patty Teramoto, Rebecca Wood, Sheela Bijea, Siew Chin Clark, Sonea Delvon, Thuan Doan, Tracey Drew, and Valerie Pollard.

the basics

yarn and tools

choosing
yarn

Choosing yarn is a lot of fun. But the combinations of fiber, color, and thickness can make it a bit overwhelming. Here are a few tips to simplify your choice and get you off to a great start.

80% wool 20% acrylic
50 g / 1.8 oz 100 m / 109 yds

4 in/10 cm
4 in/10 cm
28 rows
21 sts

4
MEDIUM

US 7 (4 mm)   G (4 mm)

When you're looking for yarn, you'll hear a lot of terminology thrown around. Yarn jargon can confuse even the most experienced knitter, but don't worry: You'll get the hang of it in no time.

A lot of what you need to know about a yarn is on its label. When choosing yarn, the three main things to pay attention to are:

• **Yarn weight:** the thickness of the yarn.

• **Gauge (tension):** the approximate size of the stitches that this yarn will make.

• **Fiber content:** what the yarn is made from.

I recommend starting with a medium-weight wool or wool blend. That is, look for a yarn weight of medium, worsted, aran, or 10-ply, and a gauge (tension) of about 16–20 stitches over 4 inches (10cm). For fiber content, wool or wool blends are good choices for learning. Wool comes in several types; superwash, merino, and lambswool are a few. Wool has a little bounce to it, making it easier to work with. Alternatively, you can work with cotton or acrylic yarn. Try to avoid yarn with a lot of texture, or yarn that is slippery.

The label also tells you care instructions, amount of yarn in the ball or skein in both ounces (grams) and yards (meters).

How to wind a skein

1

Some yarn comes in a coiled loop, called a *skein* or *hank*. You have to wind the yarn into a ball before you can use it.

2

Open the skein carefully. Ask someone to hold it open loosely for you with two hands, or hook it over the back of a chair.

3

Find the end of the yarn, and start by wrapping it around three or four of your fingers several times.

4

Carefully remove these loops from your fingers, and wrap the yarn around the middle several times. This forms the core of the ball.

5

Now wind around the core, building up evenly in all directions to make a ball. Don't wind tightly, or you'll stretch the yarn.

To prevent winding too tightly, keep your thumb under a few strands at a time as you wind.

yarn
fibers

Half the fun of learning about yarn is expanding your yarn collection, aka, your "stash." Growing a stash of yarn can be one of the most enjoyable parts of knitting. But where do you begin? First, let's take a closer look at yarn fiber.

Not that long ago, knitters were mostly limited to wool, rayon, and acrylic. Now, knitters can choose from a dizzying range of fibers and blends, from the highly exotic to the highly synthetic. The variety is wonderful, but it can be a little baffling, too. Here are some of the yarns you're likely to find, on their own or blended, starting with animal fibers:

Wool is a natural animal fiber spun from the fleece of sheep. Wool is warm, fairly elastic, lightweight, and comes in a variety of textures. It can be fine and soft, or coarse and rough. Wool is feltable, unless it's labeled superwash. It's often affordable, durable, and a great choice for the new knitter.

Here are some wool variations you might see:

Merino wool comes from the Merino breed of sheep and is one of the softest wools. Types of Merino include fine, superfine, extrafine, supersoft, and New Zealand.

Shetland wool comes from the Shetland breed of sheep. It's fine and soft.

Peruvian or Peruvian Highland wool comes from the Peruvian Highland sheep, a cross between Merino and Corriedale sheep. It's fairly soft and usually economical.

Lambswool is the wool from a young sheep.

Virgin wool is a grade of wool meaning the wool comes from the lamb's very first shearing.

Superwash wool is wool that's been treated or coated to prevent it from felting in the wash. It's generally softer than untreated wool, but it's not as elastic after washing.

Alpaca is a natural animal fiber. Alpaca fiber is long and fine, and it can be slightly hairy-looking. It's warm and soft, and varieties like baby, suri, and royal alpaca are very fine and soft to the skin. Alpaca contains no lanolin, so it's a nice alternative to wool for someone with a lanolin allergy.

Ever wondered about the difference between a llama and an alpaca? Alpacas are smaller and are raised specifically for their fleece.

Llama is a natural animal fiber, related to alpaca. When llama fiber is used in knitting yarn, it is usually selected from special breeds with very soft fleece. Baby llama and royal llama, for example, are quite luxurious.

Cashmere is a coveted natural animal fiber from the undercoat of the Cashmere (Kashmir) goat. It's very light, delicate, and soft. Cashmere is lovely to work with, but it can be expensive and a little fragile in its pure form, so look for it blended with other fibers.

Mohair is a natural animal fiber from the hair of the Angora goat. (Angora fiber, on the other hand, comes from the Angora rabbit.) Mohair has long, light fibers with a hairy texture. Its softness varies widely; kid mohair is usually the softest. When knitted loosely, the long fibers make a semiopaque and lightweight, but warm, fabric.

Angora is a natural animal fiber from the hair of the Angora *rabbit*—not to be confused with mohair, which comes from the Angora *goat!* Angora is downy soft and very fine, and it's usually blended with other fibers.

Silk is a natural animal fiber spun from the cocoons of silkworms. The texture of silk depends on how the fiber is processed, and the finish ranges from matte and rough to glossy and smooth. Pure silk can be costly, requires careful handling, and can be very heavy. Silk blends, however, are usually very nice to work with.

Camel is a natural animal fiber from the undercoat of the Bactrian camel. Camel fiber is often left in its undyed, tan-colored state. It's lightweight, very fine, soft, and luxurious.

Opossum is a natural animal fiber from the fur of opossums. Opossum fiber, like camel fiber, has a natural tint to it. It's very soft to the skin and warm.

In the plant fiber department, you'll often find the following:

Cotton is a natural vegetable fiber made from the cotton plant. Cotton is typically more dense and less elastic than wool, and the texture ranges from rough to glossy. Cotton is known for its durability and washability, and it's a nice fiber for warm weather. It has lovely stitch definition when knitted, but pure cotton can be a bit unforgiving to the new knitter, and some knitters find it hard on the hands. Cotton does really well when it lends its qualities to a fiber blend. Variations of cotton include pima, which is soft and velvety; Egyptian, which is smooth and glossy; and mercerized, which is shiny.

Hemp is a natural plant fiber from the hemp plant. Hemp is very strong and inelastic, with a matte and highly textured finish—much like linen. Pure hemp can be a little challenging to work with and hard on the hands, but it's great blended with other fibers.

Linen is a natural plant fiber made from flax. Linen has a matte and slightly grassy appearance, and it's inelastic. A wonderful fiber for warm weather, linen is often machine washable and dryable. But like other plant fibers, such as cotton and hemp, it can be a little hard on the hands, so look for a blend.

Rayon, viscose rayon, and **viscose "derived from"** are all semisynthetic fibers spun from chemically treated and extracted plant cellulose or proteins. Variations of rayon include soy, bamboo, milk, and corn. Rayon has a heavy, silky feel, and it's sometimes shiny. Pure rayon yarn is challenging to work with, but it adds luster and drape to a fiber blend.

Bamboo is usually a type of rayon derived from bamboo.

Now, for the synthetics:

Acrylic is a synthetic polymer fiber made from polyacrylonitrile and is known for its affordability and washability. It comes in a wide variety of textures and colors and is soft to the touch. When blended with other fibers, acrylic adds lightness and durability. Be careful when blocking acrylic because it flattens easily.

Nylon is synthetic polymer fiber derived from petroleum. Nylon is often blended with other yarns to add durability, particularly in sock yarn.

Polyester is a synthetic polymer fiber derived from petroleum. Polyester is a versatile fiber, and you'll often see it in novelty yarns or in blends to add texture or sheen.

Donegal tweed, when listed in the fiber content of yarn, is usually a synthetic fiber slub blended into yarn to make it look like the richly textured wools produced in Donegal, Ireland.

weights
yarn

As you expand your knitting skills, you'll want to experiment with different yarn weights. Yarn weight is a critical part of a knitting project because it affects the size of the stitches and the thickness of the knitting.

Yarn weight terminology can be confusing. Sock yarn is usually fingering weight, but it doesn't have to be used for socks only. DK means "double-knit," but does that mean it needs to be knit twice? (No.) And an aran sweater doesn't have to be made with aran-weight yarn.

If you're choosing yarn to go with a specific pattern, make note of the yarn weight given in the pattern's yarn requirements section. You don't have to buy the exact same brand and color used in the pattern, but you should look for something in the same weight, or thickness.

If you're buying yarn without a specific pattern in mind, you can buy whichever yarn most appeals to you. But remember that the finer the yarn, the more stitches you'll have to knit. Also, check the label for the recommended needle size, and purchase those too if you need them.

Below is a quick visual of the most common yarn weights.

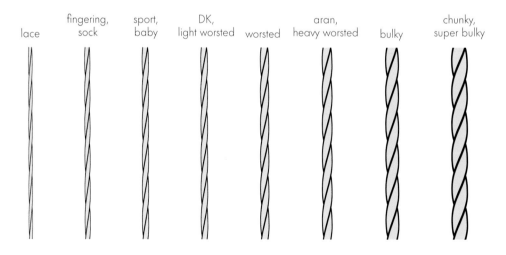

| lace | fingering, sock | sport, baby | DK, light worsted | worsted | aran, heavy worsted | bulky | chunky, super bulky |

need?

Knitting patterns usually specify how much of what yarn you need. But if you want to use a different yarn than the one suggested in the pattern, it's good to know roughly how much yarn is needed for different types of knitted items.

The following table gives some yarn guidelines for a variety of projects. Remember, these amounts are *approximate;* the true amount you need depends on the actual measurements, the amount of texture, and the gauge (tension).

Item	Size	Approximate Amount Needed		
		Fingering	**DK**	**Worsted (Aran)**
Cowl	About 45 inches (114cm) around	600 yards (548.5m)	500 yards (457m)	400 yards (366m)
Hat	Adult medium	220 yards (201m)	200 yards (183m)	170 yards (155.5m)
Scarf	About 65 inches (165cm) long	400 yards (366m)	350 yards (320m)	300 yards (274.5m)
Shawl	About 60 inches (152cm) wide	750 yards (686m)	600 yards (548.5m)	500 yards (457m)
Sweater	Infant, 6 months	350 yards (320m)	300 yards (274.5m)	250 yards (228.5m)
Sweater	Toddler, 2 years	400 yards (366m)	350 yards (320m)	300 yards (274.5m)
Sweater	Women's medium	1,500 yards (1,371.5m)	1,300 yards (1,189m)	1,100 yards (1,006m)
Sweater	Men's large	1,900 yards (1,737.5m)	1,700 yards (1,554.5m)	1,500 yards (1,371.5m)
Vest	Women's medium	800 yards (731.5m)	700 yards (640m)	600 yards (548.5m)
Vest	Men's large	1,100 yards (1,006m)	1,000 yards (914.5m)	900 yards (823m)

the right tools

Knitting is a wonderfully lightweight and economical craft. All you need to get started is some yarn and a pair of knitting needles.

But you'll also want to gather a basic kit of other useful tools. You'll use everything in this list somewhere in this book. (There are a few specialized tools I'm not mentioning here, like cable needles for making cables. Don't worry about those yet. I talk about them later when I introduce special techniques.)

Knitting Needles

Treat yourself to a good pair of knitting needles. Learning to knit with bent, dull, or rough needles is frustrating. Your needles don't have to cost much, but they should feel good in your hands.

What size? Needle size refers to the thickness of the needle. The size is listed in U.S., UK, and/or metric measures.

The thickness of the yarn you use determines what size needles you should use. All yarns work with a range of needle sizes. For example, if you're using a medium-weight yarn (worsted or aran), you can use needles ranging from U.S. 6 (4mm/UK 8) to U.S. 9 (5.5mm/UK 5).

Check your yarn label for the recommended needle size. If you can't find this information, or you're not sure, start with a pair of U.S. 7 (4.5mm/UK 7) needles.

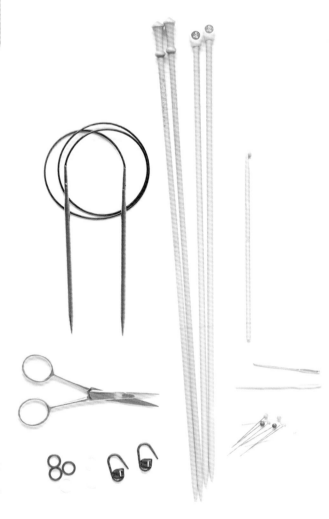

The following table shows some yarn weights and their corresponding needle sizes. Remember, these sizes are starting points. You can use slightly smaller or larger needles if you want.

Yarn Weight	Needle Size		
	U.S.	Metric	UK
super fine/sock/3-ply	2	3mm	11
fine/sport/4-ply	4	3.5mm	9
light/DK/8-ply	6	4mm	8
medium/worsted/aran/10-ply	8	5mm	6
bulky/chunky/12-ply	10	6mm	4

Straight or circular? Straight knitting needles come in pairs. They're pointed at one end with a stopper at the other. Circular needles are shorter than straight needles and are connected by a flexible cable. Either is suitable for learning. However, circulars have less needle length to hold on to so I recommend straight needles.

Which material? Knitting needles come in metal, wood, bamboo, or plastic. You'll develop your own personal preferences—so don't overthink it for now. Just be sure the needles you choose are smooth and straight.

Needle Gauge

A needle gauge is a measuring tool with different-size holes in it to measure your knitting needles. To use, insert a needle through the different holes on the needle gauge until you find the closest fit.

Crochet Hook

A crochet hook is perfect for fixing dropped stitches and making single-stitch chains.

Measuring Tape

You'll need a flexible sewing tape to take measurements.

Blunt Yarn Needle

Also called a *tapestry needle*, this needle is thick and strong with a large eye and a blunt tip. It can be metal or plastic.

Pins

Be sure your kit includes a few—about 20—straight, rustproof pins.

Scissors

Keep a pair of scissors in your kit. Small, sharp, and pointy is what you need.

Stitch Markers

Just like a bookmark, a stitch marker is a way to remember your place or remind you to come back and do something later. They come in different shapes, colors, and materials, but for the projects in this book, a few simple ring markers will do.

holding the
needles

Regardless of whether you're left- or right-handed, you're going to start by holding the yarn in your right hand. You'll often hold the yarn and a needle in one hand at the same time. If you've never knit before, this multitasking takes a little practice before it feels comfortable. There are no hard-and-fast rules here, so find what works best for *you*.

Hold one knitting needle in each hand, with the points facing each other. Keep your hands relaxed.

getting
comfortable

Knitting should be a pleasure, not a strain.

Find a well-lit place to sit, like an armchair with a lamp beside it. You want enough room for your needles and elbows, and you need enough light to see this book and your knitting clearly. If someone is helping you, sitting side by side on a sofa is great. Or while you're learning new techniques, you might find it helpful to sit at a table with your forearms resting on the table with your yarn in front of you.

It's important to avoid undue strain on your eyes, neck, shoulders, wrists, and hands as you knit. While you're intently looking at your knitting, you might find you've bent over your work, your shoulders are tense, or you're squinting at your stitches. The solution is easy, and is true for knitters at any level: take a break! Stand up, shake out any tension, and focus your eyes on something else for a few minutes before you come back to your knitting.

- -

Knit in a well-lit spot. It's a good idea to have your scissors, a notepad, and a pencil close at hand, too.

- -

start knitting

casting on

Casting on is where it all begins. When you cast on, you make a row of loops on your needle. This row of loops, or stitches, is the foundation for your knitting.

There are many different ways to cast on. We start with one of the easiest methods, called a *half-hitch* cast-on.

The Slipknot

Start with a slipknot. You've probably made a slipknot before without thinking about it, but here it is step by step.

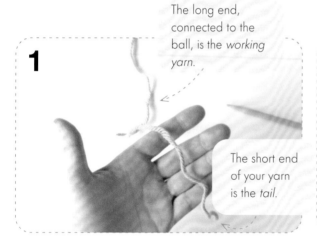

1 The long end, connected to the ball, is the *working yarn*.

The short end of your yarn is the *tail*.

Drape the working yarn over the fingers of your left hand, with the tail hanging in front.

2 Using your thumb, hold the yarn tail to the inside of your fingers, and wrap the working yarn (highlighted red in the photo) once around your fingers.

3

Carefully slide the loop off your fingers, keeping it closed at the top.

4

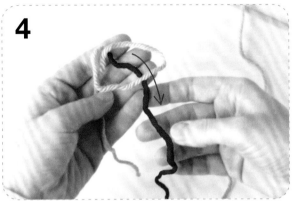

Take the working yarn down and behind the loop.

5

Put a knitting needle under the strand of yarn you just put behind the loop.

6

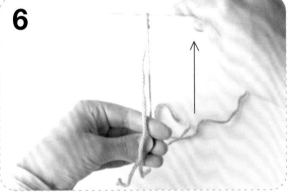

Holding both the tail and the working yarn, pull the needle up to tighten the loop. Then pull the working yarn to draw the knot up to the needle.

The Half-Hitch Cast-On

Let's try casting on 20 stitches. Start with a slipknot.

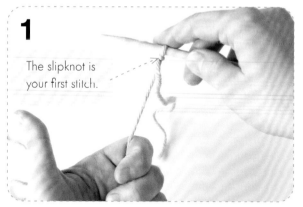

The slipknot is your first stitch.

Hold the needle with the slipknot in your right hand. Hold the working yarn in your left hand, keeping your thumb free. It's going to do most of the work.

Put your thumb behind the yarn.

Hook the yarn with your thumb. You'll look like you're giving a thumbs-up.

Put the needle tip near the crook of your thumb, under the strand of yarn closest to you.

5

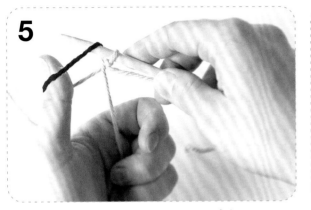

Lift up the strand, being careful not to catch the strand in the back.

6

Pull out your thumb.

7

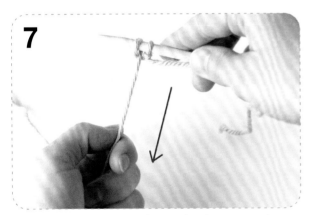

Pull the yarn to tighten the loop on the needle. That's your cast-on stitch!

8

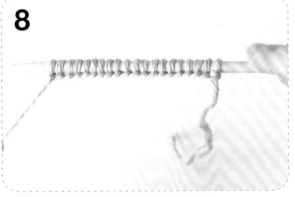

Repeat steps 1 through 7 until you have 20 stitches.

the knit stitch

No matter how sophisticated your knitting skills get, you'll never stray far from the basic knit stitch. It's the foundation for all your knitting.

The yarn tail is on the left; the working yarn is on the right.

Cast on 10 stitches. Hold the needle with the stitches in your left hand. Put the tip of the right needle to the left of the first stitch ...

... and then insert the needle, front to back, through the stitch. Your needles will form an X, with your left needle on top.

Pick up the yarn with your right hand.

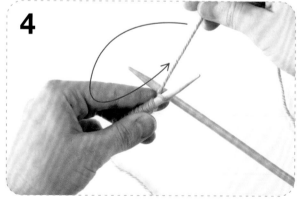

Wrap the yarn once, counterclockwise, around your right needle. Don't let go of the yarn yet.

5

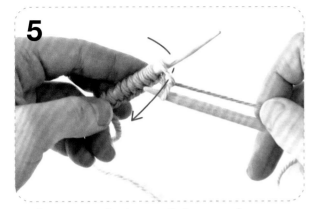

This is a tricky bit: pull the tip of your right needle back out through the stitch, bringing the wrapped yarn with it.

6

With the tip of your left finger, carefully slide the first stitch off the left needle.

7

The stitch should be snug enough it doesn't fall off, but with enough slack that you can slide it on the needle.

Gently pull the yarn to barely tighten it on the right needle. You can let go of the yarn now.

8

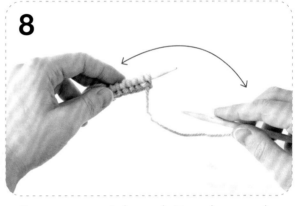

Repeat steps 1 through 7 until no stitches remain on your left needle. You've knit your first row! Swap needles, with the working yarn on the right, and you're ready to start another row.

Keep knitting rows the same way, repeating steps 1 through 7 for each stitch. After a few rows, you'll have something called *garter stitch.* Don't worry about making your stitches perfect right now. Just focus on getting familiar with the motions.

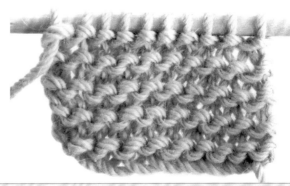

the purl stitch

The front of the basic stitch is the *knit*, and the flip side is the *purl*.

When you learned the knit stitch, you also learned how to make *garter* stitch fabric. This time, as you learn the purl stitch, you're going to learn how to make *stockinette*, or *stocking*, stitch.

1

Cast on 10 stitches and knit 1 row. Hold the stitches in your left hand, with the working yarn on the right.

2

Put the tip of the right needle into the front of the first stitch, right to left. Your needles make an X, with the right needle in front.

3

Notice that when you purl, your yarn is at the front, but when you knit, it's at the back.

With your right hand, pick up the yarn from the front ...

4

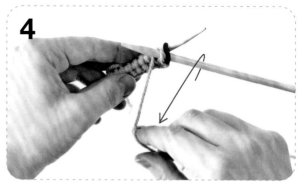

... and wrap it counterclockwise around the right needle.

5

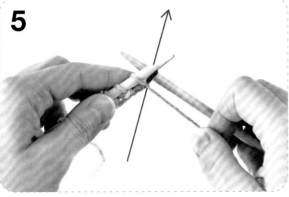

With the tip of your right needle, carefully catch the wrapped yarn and pull it through to the back.

6

Carefully slide the first stitch on the left needle off.

7

Pull the working yarn to tighten the stitch on the needle, just as you did with the knit stitch.

8

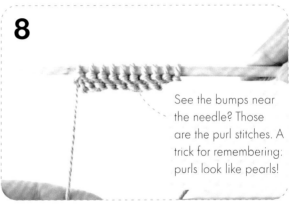

See the bumps near the needle? Those are the purl stitches. A trick for remembering: purls look like pearls!

Continue repeating these steps until you've purled all the stitches.

After you finish a row of purls, swap your needles and knit a row. When you alternate knit rows and purl rows, you get stockinette (stocking) stitch.

The right—and smoothest—side of this fabric looks like rows of Vs. ▶

together

By learning the knit and the purl stitch, you have unlocked an infinite number of knitted textures. You don't have to keep knits on one side and purls on the other. You can mix them up!

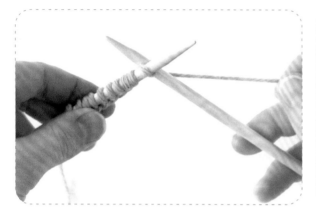

You've probably noticed that when you're about to *knit*, the yarn is at the *back*.

And when you're about to *purl*, the yarn is at the *front*.

Let's learn a new stitch pattern, called *ribbing,* to figure out how to mix knits and purls together on the same row, and how to get the yarn where you need it.

Ribbing: Mixing Knits and Purls

You see knitted ribbing everywhere. Look closely at the cuffs of sweaters, sweatshirts, socks, hats, or mittens, and you'll see ribbing. Elastic and durable, ribbing is the most versatile of knitted borders. Try pulling it; it stretches horizontally and doesn't curl at the cast-on edge.

Now let's learn knit 1, purl 1 ribbing (also called *1/1* or *K1/P1 ribbing*). I've started off with a few rows of ribbing already on the needles so it's a little easier for you to see where we're heading. Get your needles and yarn set up to knit.

1

Knit 1 stitch. Notice that your yarn is at the back of your work.

2

The next stitch will be a purl, so bring the yarn from the back, between the tips of your needles, and to the front.

3

Purl 1 stitch. Notice your yarn is at the front of your work.

4

Take the yarn between the needles to the back, and now you're ready to knit.

Repeat these steps until you complete the row. Work the next row the same way, but start with a purl stitch: purl 1 stitch, take your yarn to the back, knit 1 stitch, bring your yarn to the front, and repeat.

If the stitch looks like a flat V, knit it. If it has a bump, purl it.

How to "Read" Your Knitting

When you're combining knits and purls, knitting gets more complicated than plain stockinette (stocking) or garter stitch, and you have to keep careful track of which comes next, knit or purl. In other words, you need to "read" your knitting.

Let's check out some quick stitch anatomy. The essence of the stitch is a loop. Think of the top of the loop as the *head,* and the two sides as its *legs.*

How a stitch is connected to the stitch above it is what makes it look like a knit or a purl.

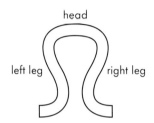

A knit goes over the loop above it with its head at the back and its legs showing. It looks like a V.

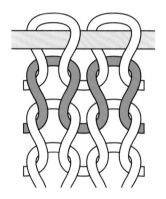

A purl goes over the loop with its head in front and its legs hidden. It looks like a bump.

And of course, remember that a purl is the back of a knit and vice versa. You can think of the stitch as a small child sitting on his or her parent's shoulders: whether you see the child's legs (a knit) or the back of his or her head (a purl) depends on whether you're looking from the front or back.

Notice, too, that the right leg of the stitch is always on top of the needle (unless the stitch is twisted—more on that later).

What Did I Just Do?

Check the front of the stitch. Is there a bump right next to the needle on the front? If so, you just made a purl. No bump? Then it's a knit.

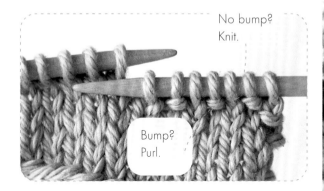

No bump? Knit.

Bump? Purl.

The same rule applies when you wonder, **What's coming next?** You often know where you are in a row by the stitches on the previous row—that is, the stitches you see on the left needle. Again, check the front of the stitch. Bump? Purl. No bump? Knit.

better
cast-ons

The half-hitch cast-on is great because it's fast and easy to learn. However, there are three other cast-on methods that make a more refined edge to your knitting.

Knitted Cast-On

This cast-on makes a slightly open cast-on edge and is a nice method for beginners because it has the same movements as the knit stitch.

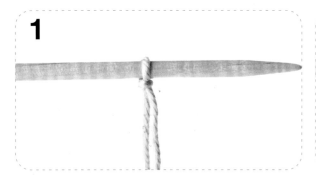

1

Start with a slipknot on your left needle. This is your first stitch.

2

With your right needle, knit 1 stitch but don't slide the loop off the left needle.

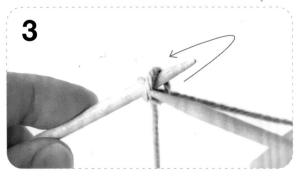

3

Place the loop you just made back on your left needle.

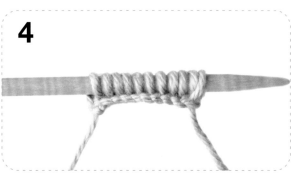

4

Repeat steps 2 and 3 until you have the desired number of stitches on your left needle.

Cable Cast-On

A natural step after learning the knitted cast-on, the cable cast-on makes a firmer edge.

Make a slipknot and cast on 1 stitch using the knitted cast-on.

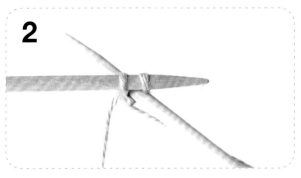

Put your right needle between the first 2 stitches on your left needle.

Wrap the yarn around your right needle, and pull through.

Place the loop you just made back on your left needle.

Repeat steps 2 through 4 until you have the desired number of stitches.

Long Tail Cast-On

A popular and versatile cast-on, this method takes some concentration to learn because you work with two strands of yarn at once. It's related to the half-hitch cast-on and uses the same movements but with some extra complexity: instead of making half-hitch loops over the needle, you make them over a second strand of yarn. As the name suggests, you start with a long tail of yarn.

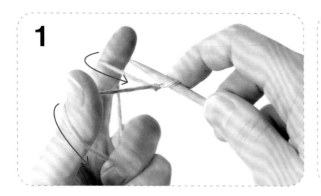

Start with a slipknot on your right needle, leaving a tail of yarn four times as long as the desired width of your cast-on. In your left hand, hold the tail going over your thumb and the working yarn over your index finger. Hold the needle in your right hand.

With the tip of your needle, catch and lift up the strand closest to you. You might notice this is like the half-hitch.

If your knitting will be 12 inches (30cm) wide, leave a tail 48 inches (120cm) long. When in doubt, make the tail longer than you think you'll need. It's much better to overestimate the length of the tail than have it too short.

3

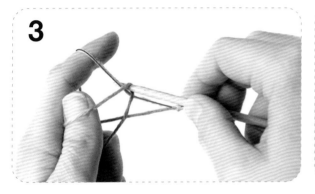

Without dropping the yarn from your thumb, put the needle tip over the back of the strand that's sitting on your index finger ...

4

... and pull it through the space next to your thumb and up to form a stitch.

5

Let the yarn drop off your thumb, and pull the tail end down to tighten the stitch.

6

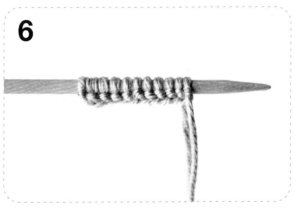

Reposition the tail over your thumb, and repeat.

The long-tail cast-on edge, when you start your first row, looks like a row of purls. Some knitters choose to purl one row before starting their pattern.

basic finishing

binding off
(casting off)

If you ever pull your knitting off the needle, you'll notice that the loops unravel very easily. Binding off, or casting off, is how you secure your final row of stitches and get it off the needle.

Let's learn the most frequently used bind (cast) off: the knitwise bind (cast) off.

1

Try to knit the stitches a little more loosely than you usually would.

Knit 2 stitches.

2

Put the left needle tip into the front of the stitch on the right.

3

Lift this stitch carefully over its neighbor ...

4

... and off the needle, making sure not to knock off the first stitch!

5

Knit another stitch, and repeat the previous 3 steps until 1 stitch remains on the left needle. Loosen the last stitch a little.

6

Drop the stitch from the needle, and cut the working yarn, leaving a tail.

7

Push the tail through the last stitch, back to the front, and pull it gently to close the stitch.

8

Your bound (cast) off edge looks like a tidy chain of stitches.

Sometimes you'll want a purlwise bind (cast) off. You work this almost exactly the same as the knitwise bind (cast) off, except you purl instead of knit.

The top shows a knitwise; the bottom shows a purlwise bind (cast) off. ▷

weaving in and blocking

Finishing in knitting is just what it sounds like: You tidy up all the loose ends to make the knitting look clean and polished. You also ensure nothing will unravel.

Weaving In

You hide and secure the yarn tails by threading them through the backs of existing stitches. This is called *weaving in*. You'll need a thick, blunt needle with an eye wide enough to fit the yarn through.

The easiest way to hide your yarn tails is by threading them in and out of the back of the stitches at the edge of your knitting. (I share some other weaving-in tricks later.)

Lay your knitting flat with the wrong side facing you. (If your knitting is reversible, either side will do.)

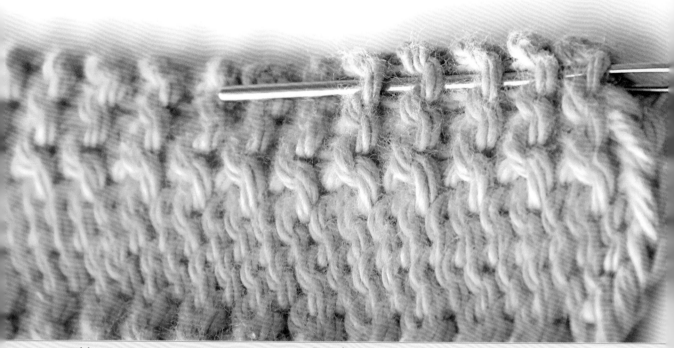

1

Thread your yarn tail through the needle. Look at the edge and find the bumps of the stitches.

2

Thread your needle in and out through the back of about 5 of these bumps. Don't *pierce* the yarn. Thread the needle *under* it instead.

3

On the way back, don't thread through this stitch.

Then thread the needle back the other way through the same bumps, skipping the first one.

4

Snip the yarn about $\frac{1}{8}$ inch (0.3cm) away from your knitting. Be careful not to nick the fabric!

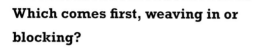

Which comes first, weaving in or blocking?

You'll get different advice on this question, but either way works. When possible, I prefer to leave weaving in to the very end. It's a satisfying way to finish a project, but also (if done well) very hard to undo. I also find that blocking before weaving makes it easier to see the backs of stitches to weave into.

Basic Blocking

A piece of knitting fresh off the needles isn't always the exact shape you want it to be. And sometimes your stitches might look a little uneven. That's where *blocking* comes in. With blocking, you use pins, heat, and/or moisture to straighten edges, smooth out uneven spots, and get your piece into shape. We look at blocking in more detail later, but here's a good basic blocking method. You'll need pins, a ruler, a spray bottle with water, and a clean dry towel.

Lay your knitting flat, right side up, on the towel. Mist it with water. You're aiming for moist, not soaked.

Gently pull the piece in all directions, smoothing it out and squaring the corners.

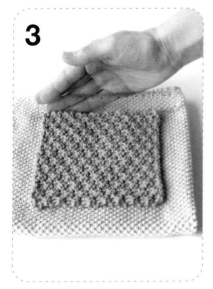

Nudge the edges straight with your ruler.

Pin along the edges in several spots, and allow to dry.

beginner practice projects

garter stitch
washcloth

Every knitter starts with the humble square. Actually, I started with an accidental *triangle* because my tension progressed from very loose to very tight as I learned to knit! It's easy to turn your knitted square into a sweet gift: a knitted washcloth. Make a few of these, fold them neatly, and bundle them together with a pretty bar of soap for a much-appreciated gift!

Yarn

About 60 yards (55m) cotton or cotton blend, in a lightweight (light worsted or double knit) yarn.

Needles

U.S. 6 (4mm/UK 8) straight needles

Other Supplies

Blunt yarn needle, scissors, measuring tape, pins

Bind (cast) off. Cut the yarn, leaving a tail. You now have a squarish piece with two tails.

Finishing

Lay your washcloth on a clean towel, dampen it with a spray bottle full of water or a moist cloth, pin it into a square, and allow it to dry.

Thread one of the tails on the blunt needle, and weave it in. Do the same for the other tail. Snip off the tails close to the knitting.

Garter Stitch Washcloth

Cast on 34 stitches. Remember to leave a tail about 6 inches (15cm) long to weave in later.

Knit 50 rows. You can count how many rows you've done by looking at the ridges you make: each ridge is 2 rows, so knit until you have 25 ridges.

Put your work on a flat surface, measure the width of your knitting, and write down that number. It will be approximately 6 or 7 inches (15 to 18cm). Now measure the height of your knitting from the cast-on edge to your needle. Your goal is to knit until the height is the same as the width so you have a square washcloth.

Keep knitting and measuring the height, a couple rows at a time, until the height matches the width.

This is a garter stitch "ridge."

chevron coaster

Try out some texture with these pretty coasters. Bundle a few of these for a lovely gift. Ever wondered about the word *chevron?* It refers to patterns or insignia made of *V*s or inverted *V* shapes, but it actually shares the origins of the French word for goat! The word itself was used to describe *V*-shape roof tiles, which were compared to the shape of a goat's hind legs.

Skills Needed

Combining knits and purls

Finished Measurements

About 3 × 3 inches (7.5 × 7.5cm)

Yarn

About 30 yards (27.5m) medium-weight (worsted or aran) yarn.

Gauge (Tension)

20 stitches = 4 inches (10cm) in stockinette (stocking) stitch. Gauge (tension) isn't crucial for this project.

Needles

U.S. 6 (4mm/UK 8) straight or circular needles

Other Supplies

Blunt yarn needle

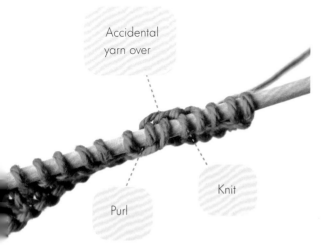

Accidental yarn over

Purl

Knit

Chevron Coaster

Cast on 17 stitches.

Row 1 (Right Side): Purl 1, knit 7, purl 1, knit 7, purl 1.

Row 2 (Wrong Side): Knit 2, purl 5, knit 3, purl 5, knit 2.

Row 3: Knit 1, purl 2, knit 3, purl 2; repeat that sequence; end with knit 1.

Row 4: Purl 2, knit 2, purl 1, knit 2, purl 1; repeat that sequence; end with purl 1.

Row 5: Knit 3, purl 1, knit 1, purl 1, knit 2; repeat that sequence; end with knit 1.

Row 6: Purl across.

Repeat Rows 1 through 6 twice more.

Repeat Rows 1 through 5 once.

Bind (cast) off.

Finishing

Block your coaster, and weave in the ends.

- -

As you finish each row, count your stitches. One common problem when combining knits and purls is that the yarn goes *over* the right needle instead of *between* the two needles when you take it to the back or front. If that happens, you'll find an extra strand that looks like a stitch. Don't panic—just slide the extra strand off the needle when you come to it on the next row.

- -

beyond the basics

knitting evenly

gauge
(tension)

Knitting gauge, or tension, is key to the finished measurements of all your knitting and refers to the width and height of each stitch. Gauge (tension) is often expressed in number of stitches and rows in a 1-inch (2.5cm) or 4-inch (10cm) square. Although gauge (tension) is partly determined by yarn thickness and needle size, it varies from knitter to knitter.

Suggested

Most yarn labels list a *suggested* gauge (tension) the average knitter can achieve using the recommended needle size. This is a guideline to help you choose the right yarn for your pattern and the right needles for your yarn. But remember, treat this as a guideline only. Never assume your actual gauge will be the same as what's listed on the yarn label.

Required

Almost all patterns list the *required* gauge (tension) to achieve the desired finished measurements. Often, gauge (tension) isn't crucial, such as when you're knitting a scarf. But for any project where you need an accurate fit, it's essential.

Actual

To measure gauge (tension), start by knitting a square using the recommended needle size. Cast on enough stitches to make a square more than 4 inches (10cm) wide to give you the most accurate measure.

To calculate how many stitches to cast on, check the suggested gauge on the yarn label. For example, a medium weight (worsted or aran) might say $4\frac{1}{2}$ to 5 stitches per 1 inch (2.5cm). Aiming for a 5-inch (13cm) square, multiply the higher end of the range (5 stitches) by the target width of your square: 5 stitches × 5 inches = 25, so cast on 25 stitches.

Work enough rows to make a square and bind (cast) off. Unless the pattern specifies otherwise, work in stockinette (stocking) stitch. Some patterns may specify gauge (tension) *in pattern*. In those cases, work in the stitch pattern or texture used in the pattern.

For accuracy, take the time to block your swatch. Many fibers stretch or shrink in water!

First measure horizontally across a row, noting the number of stitches that fit in 4 inches (10cm).

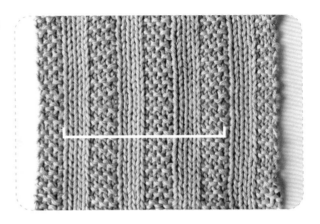

Then, count vertically the number of rows that fit in 4 inches (10cm).

In this example, there are 17.5 stitches and 26 rows in 4 inches (10cm).

joining
new yarn

You've come to the end of a ball of yarn. Now what? Here are three simple ways to join new yarn.

At the Beginning of a Row

This is the best and simplest method. You simply drop the old yarn and start knitting with the new.

Drop the old yarn and pick up the new. After a few stitches, tie the ends together. Weave in the ends along the edge using the basic weave-in method.

In the Middle of a Row

Sometimes you have to join a new ball of yarn in the middle of a row.

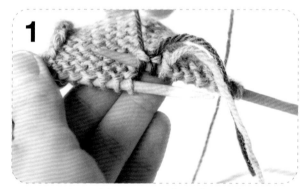

Drop the old yarn and pick up the new, leaving both ends hanging on the back of your work.

After a few stitches, tie the ends together. Weave in the ends using duplicate stitch weaving.

Felted Join

This method only works for feltable animal fiber, but it is ideal. You actually graft the end of the old ball to the beginning of the new ball. The method is also called *spit grafting*.

Hold the two ends in your palm, parallel to each other, and heading in opposite directions. Moisten the ends with a spray bottle. (Or you can lick your palm—that's why it's called spit grafting!)

Rub the two ends together firmly but gently. The idea is to felt the fibers together slightly using pressure, moisture, and heat.

The two ends will be seamlessly joined (with a slight bulge), and once you knit in the graft, it'll be secure and mostly invisible.

yarn

Once you're comfortable with your needles, you'll want to experiment with how you hold your yarn. Experienced knitters often weave the yarn over and under their fingers, keeping it slightly taut. This makes the knitting faster and the gauge (tension) more consistent. It might feel awkward at first, but don't worry, you'll master it with practice.

Every knitter's yarn-holding method is slightly different, but with this basic technique, your index finger controls the knitting action while your little finger manages the yarn tension.

Why Bother?

Learning to hold the yarn like this will feel awkward at first. When I was little and learning to knit, I *loathed* learning how to hold the yarn "properly." It felt clumsy and slow to me.

But if you persevere, it is worth it. Managing the tension gives you more evenly sized and shaped stitches, and makes your gauge (tension) more consistent. And with practice, you'll become a much faster knitter.

That said, do what feels right for you. I know many knitters who, after years of knitting, pick up their yarn every time they make a stitch. They're not the fastest knitters, but they're happy, and that's what matters.

Getting Your Yarn in Position

Your little finger isn't super strong, but it's strong enough to add just enough tension to the working yarn and feed out the yarn a little bit at a time. Some people prefer to use their ring finger or their ring and little fingers together. Use whatever works best for you. Your index finger, stronger and more agile, manages the action end of the yarn close to the needles.

Here's how you get your yarn in place. This technique is the same for your left or right hand:

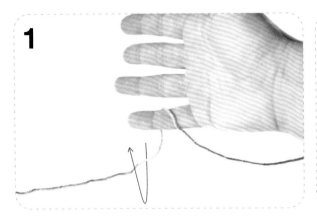

With your palm facing you, scoop up the yarn with your little finger so it goes back to front.

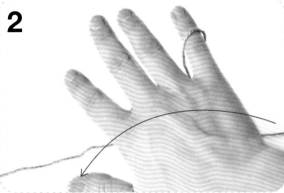

Turn your hand over, palm down, with the yarn still looped around your little finger.

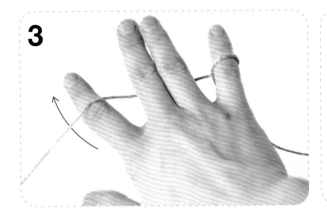

Put your index finger under the yarn, front to back.

Here's how the yarn looks on the other side.

Which Hand?

Up to now, I've been showing you to how to knit using your right hand to hold the yarn. But you can hold your yarn in either hand.

In Your Right Hand

When you hold the yarn in your right hand, the index finger on your right hand dominates the action. Most of the movement is in your right hand and right needle, with your left hand doing a lot of support, stabilizing needles, and pushing stitches to the tip. Whether knitting or purling, your right index finger wraps the yarn around the needle tip, and your right hand manipulates the needle to pull the yarn through.

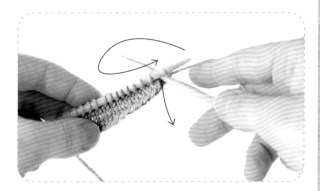

Right-handed knitting is sometimes called *English* or *throwing.* Left-handed knitting is sometimes called *Continental* or *picking.*

In Your Left Hand

Even though this looks like a mirror image of right-handed knitting, the movements are quite different. In this scenario, the right needle is in charge, hooking the yarn and pulling it through. Your left hand moves very little. Its primary job is to hold the yarn in position and stabilize the left needle. Because the yarn doesn't have to be wrapped around the needle, left-handed knitting requires small movements, making it quite efficient.

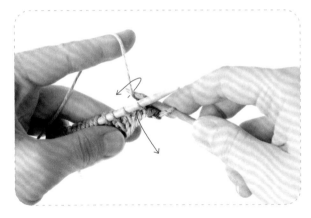

Purling with the yarn in your left hand is a little more involved. When knitting, the yarn is in the correct position by default. When purling, you need to shift down the yarn to get it in the right position to go around the needle counterclockwise. To get the yarn in the right spot, push it down with your thumb before pulling it through with the right needle.

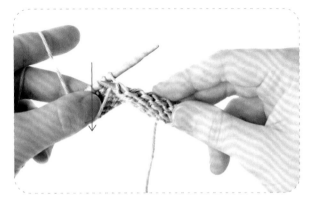

Which is better, left or right? Each method has its advantages. Try both, and do what feels best. I knit with my left hand and purl with my right.

increasing and decreasing

increasing

It's time to move beyond the rectangle! You can change the shape and size of your knitting by adding or taking away stitches at almost any point. Adding is called increasing; let's look at some commonly used increasing methods.

Yarn Over (yo)

This type of increase makes a visible hole in the knitting. The hole can be used as a buttonhole or as a decorative element in eyelets or lace. It's usually worked between 2 stitches.

1

Bring the yarn between the needles to the opposite side. For example, if you're knitting, bring it to the front.

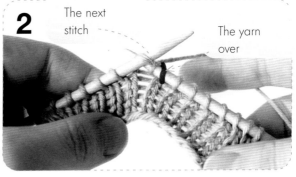

2

The next stitch — The yarn over

When you work the next stitch, the yarn has to go over the needle.

3

The completed yarn over is a strand over the needle with a gap below it.

Make 1 (m1)

This instruction, make 1 stitch, can mean more than one thing because knitting conventions vary and change over time, but here is one way to make 1. It's worked between 2 stitches.

1

Look between the left and right needles. You'll find a horizontal strand of yarn (called the running strand). Put the right needle through it, front to back.

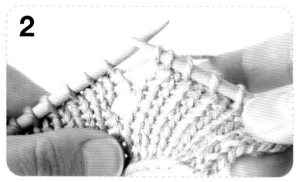

2

Wrap the yarn around the needle and pull it through, as you would to knit. This makes a new stitch on the needle above a gap.

The gap in the finished knitting will be slightly smaller than the size of a yarn over. To make 1 without the gap, see the next section.

Make 1 Left and Right (m1L, m1R)

These two types of increases are variations of make 1. They make a snug new stitch.

1

For make 1 *left*, put the left needle tip under the running strand from front to back.

2

Knit through the *back* of this strand.

This makes a new stitch above a twisted strand, leaning to the left. Notice how this make 1 does not make a gap. This is because you twist the strand by knitting into the back of it.

Now let's look at how to make a new stitch above a twisted strand leaning to the *right:*

Put the right needle tip under the running strand, from front to back.

Place it on the left needle. Notice that the left leg of this strand is at the *front.*

Knit through the *front* of the strand.

This makes a new stitch above a twisted strand, leaning to the right.

Knit Front and Back (kfb)

You make this increase just as it sounds, by working first into the front of a stitch as you normally would and then working into the back of the same stitch. Unlike the other increases you've learned, which are worked *between* 2 stitches, kfb is worked *into* a stitch.

Knit a stitch as you normally would, but don't slide the stitch off the left needle.

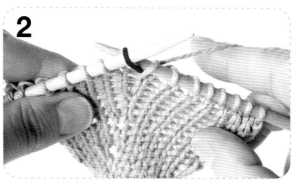

Move the right needle around to the back and put it through the back of the stitch.

Wrap the yarn around and pull it through. You'll see 2 stitches side by side on your right needle. Now slide the stitch off the left needle.

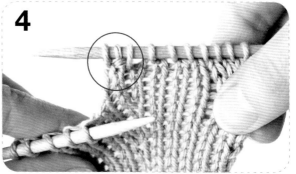

This increase makes a visible bar below the new stitch. Because of this, it's also called a *bar increase*.

If you're following a pattern, the pattern writer will usually instruct you to use a particular increase. Sometimes, though, a pattern only says "increase" and you have to choose which one to use. If you want a prominent, open increase, use a yarn over. For a subtler increase, a make 1 left or right is excellent.

decreasing

Just as adding stitches is called increasing, taking away stitches is called *decreasing.* Let's look at several methods of decreasing.

Knit 2 Together (k2tog)

This decreases 1 stitch by overlapping 2 stitches to the right.

1

Put the tip of your right needle through the first 2 stitches, just as you would to knit, treating the 2 stitches as 1.

2

Wrap the yarn around and pull through, knitting the 2 stitches together.

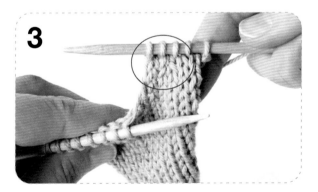

3

You can see the 2 stitches, with the leftmost on top, pulled slightly to the right below 1 stitch on the needle.

Slip-Slip-Knit (ssk)

This decrease is the left-leaning counterpart to knit 2 together, but it takes a few extra steps.

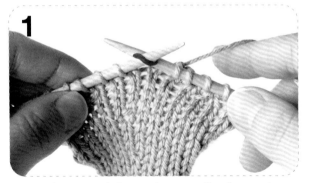

Put the tip of the right needle through the first stitch, as if to knit.

Pull the stitch onto the right needle. This is called *slipping a stitch knitwise*.

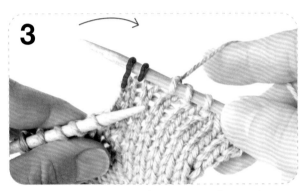

Repeat steps 1 and 2 so you have 2 slipped stitches on your right needle.

Put the left needle through the *fronts* of the slipped stitches, from left to right.

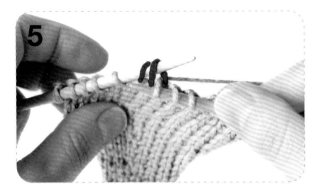

Wrap the yarn around the right needle and pull it through, as you would to knit.

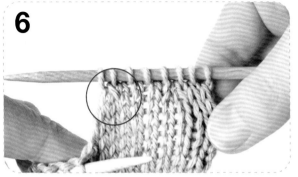

You can see the 2 stitches, leaning to the left below 1 stitch on the needle.

Slip 1, Knit 2 Together, Pass Slipped Stitch Over (sl1-k2tog-psso)

This decreases 2 stitches at once, with a decrease that leans to the left.

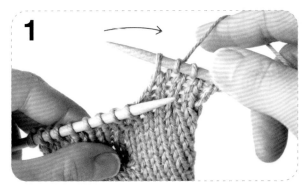

Slip 1 stitch knitwise.

Knit the next 2 stitches together.

Put the left needle tip into the front of the slipped stitch, from left to right ...

... and lift it up and over the k2tog stitch.

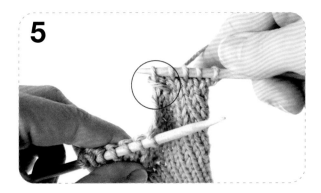

You can see the 3 stitches clustered below the new stitch on the needle, with the rightmost stitch on top.

Slip 2, Knit 1, Pass 2 Slipped Stitches Over (sl2-k1-p2sso)

This decreases 2 stitches at once, with a prominent centered decrease.

1

Put your needle through the first 2 stitches as if to knit 2 together ...

2

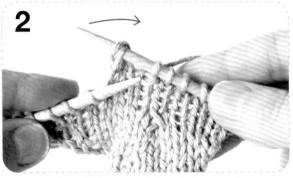

... and pull them off the left needle, transferring them to the right needle.

3

Knit 1.

4

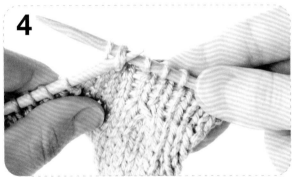

Put the left needle tip into the *front* of the 2 slipped stitches, from left to right ...

5

... and lift them up and over the knit stitch.

6

You can see 3 stitches clustered under 1 stitch, with the center stitch on top.

Knit 3 Stitches Together (k3tog)

This decreases 2 stitches at once and slants to the right.

Put your needle through the first 3 stitches from left to right, front to back.

Wrap the yarn around the needle and pull it through, as you would to knit.

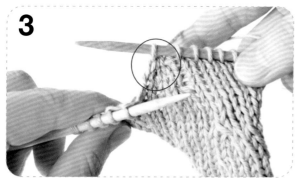

You can see 3 stitches clustered below the new stitch on the needle, with the leftmost stitch on top.

Knit-speak and shaping

When you're following a pattern and there's a change in the stitch count due to increasing or decreasing, the pattern will give you the new number of stitches you should have on your needles at the end of the row. This will be noted, usually, with a long dash followed by the new stitch count:

Cast on 20 stitches.

Row 1: Knit 2 together, k16, slip-slip-knit—18 stitches.

Decreasing on the Purl Side

You won't often have to work a decrease on the purl side of your work, unless you get into advanced lace knitting or sweater construction. However, here are two basic purled decreases you might need.

Purl 2 Together (p2tog)

This is the purl version of knit 2 together. When viewed from the right side, a p2tog looks like a k2tog.

Put your right needle, right to left, through the front of the first 2 stitches.

Wrap the yarn around the needle and purl them together.

Purl 3 Together (p3tog)

This is the purl version of knit 3 together. When viewed from the right side, a p3tog looks like a k3tog.

Put the right needle, right to left, through the front of the first 3 stitches.

Wrap the yarn around the needle and purl them together.

knitting in the round

circular
knitting methods

You've been knitting back and forth in rows, making flat pieces of knitting. If you want to knit a hat or a pair of socks, you need to know how to knit *around* instead of back and forth. You need to know how to knit a tube.

Knitting a tube is called knitting *in the round,* or *circular knitting,* and instead of rows, you knit rounds. To knit in the round, you need to use circular needles (two straight needles joined by a flexible cable) or double-pointed needles (dpn). Which ones you choose depend on the size of the tube you're knitting and your personal preference.

Circular Needles

Circular needles are available with different lengths of cable, and they're very versatile. You can use them to knit flat pieces back and forth, just like you would use straight needles. The cable lets the work sit in your lap, and the shorter needles means your project is more compact.

Circulars also enable you to work in the round on *one* set of circular needles when the round is *larger* than the total length of your needles. Or you can work in the round on *two* sets of circular needles when the round is *smaller* than the length of one set of circulars. This might sound backward, but I show you how this works in the following sections.

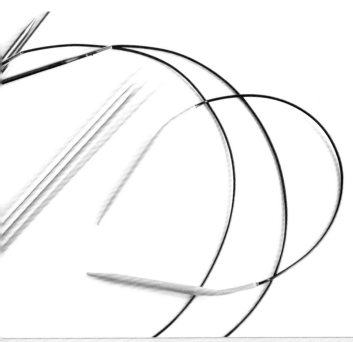

Knitting in the Round on One Set of Circular Needles

The simplest way to work in the round is with one set of circulars. But the circumference of your knitting needs to be *larger* than the circumference of your needles when held with the needle tips crossed; otherwise, the stitches will be strained. Working in the round on one set is ideal for sweaters and cowls.

Cast on the required number of stitches for your project. Arrange your stitches with the working yarn on the right needle. Carefully check all your stitches to be sure they're facing the same way and your cast-on edge doesn't twist around the needle at any point.

Ring marker

Place a ring marker over the right needle, and put the right needle through the first stitch on the left needle to knit. Check again that your cast-on edge hasn't twisted around the needle.

Knit the first stitch, and pull the yarn snug so the first stitch on the right needle and your new stitch are side by side.

Then knit normally. When you reach the marker, you'll notice a gap where you first joined in the round. After a few rounds, the gap will close.

Knitting in the Round on Two Sets of Circular Needles

This looks like a brain teaser when you first try it. It can be hard to visualize how you're going to knit in circles with two circular needles. This method is ideal for tubes that have a *smaller* circumference than one of your needles, like socks, mitts, yokes of sweaters, and sleeves. You'll need two sets of circular needles the same size.

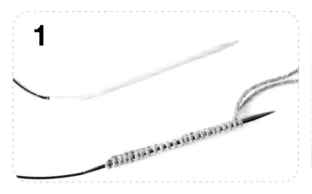

1

Cast on the required number of stitches to one of the needles.

2

Transfer half of the stitches to the second needle.

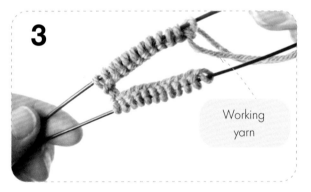

3

Working yarn

Slide the needles so the stitches are in the middle of the cables. Arrange your work so the working yarn is on the right. Carefully check all your stitches to be sure they're facing the same way and the cast-on edge isn't crossing over the cables at any point.

4

Slide the needle closest to you (the one without the working yarn) so the stitches are near the tip, ready to be worked. Let's call this the *working needle*.

5

Working needles

With the other end of the working needle, put the tip through the first stitch and wrap the stitch around to knit. Check again that your cast-on edge isn't twisted. Then knit the stitch, pulling the yarn snugly to join the gap.

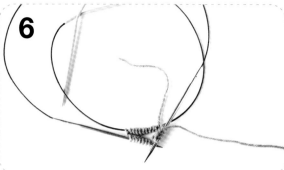

6

Continue knitting the stitches with your working needle. Here's what it looks like after a few stitches. The working yarn is on the right working needle tip, and the next stitches to be worked are on the right needle tip.

7

Knit all the stitches on the working needle. To continue your round, turn your needles over and arrange your work as it looked in step 4, with the working yarn on the right and the stitches on the front needle ready to work. When you're ready to put your knitting aside, slide the stitches to the middle of the cables so they won't drop off the tips.

At any point, there's only one working needle. The second needle just hangs there. When you finish the stitches on the working needle, the needles trade jobs—the hanging needle becomes the working needle and the old working needle takes a break.

Double-Pointed Needles

Double-pointed needles, or dpns, are straight needles with points at each end. They come in sets of 4 or 5 and are used for knitting in small rounds like with socks, sleeves, or the tops of hats. Getting your work cast on and joined is the trickier part of working with dpns. Here's a cast-on method that requires an extra needle long enough to hold all the stitches. You can use a set of 4 or 5 dpns; the technique is the same.

Cast on the required number of stitches to your extra needle.

Transfer the stitches to 3 of the 4 (or 4 of the 5) dpns, evenly distributing the stitches.

Arrange your stitches with the working yarn on the right needle. Check to be sure your stitches all face the same way and the cast-on edge doesn't twist around the needles at any point. With the empty dpn, put the needle through the first stitch on the left, ready to knit.

Wrap the yarn around the needle to knit, check again that your cast-on edge isn't twisted, and knit the stitch. Pull the yarn snug to close the gap between your needles.

5

Continue knitting across the needle. When you reach the end of the stitches on the current dpn, use the now-empty needle as your right-hand working needle.

If you twist the cast-on edge before you join in the round, you'll have a tube with one twist in it, or a Möbius strip. This might be a good demonstration of a mathematical concept, but it's not good in knitting!

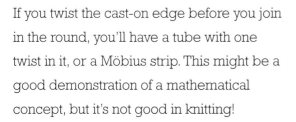

6

Here's how the tube looks after a few rounds.

color knitting

adding color with
stripes

With so many wonderful colors of yarn available, it's inevitable you'll want to try mixing them together. The simplest way to start mixing colors is with stripes. (We get to more advanced techniques later.) Stripes are so simple to work in knitting. Whether you use them a little or a lot, make them all the same width or mix them up, stripes are guaranteed to look great.

When alternating colors, make your stripes an even number of rows tall.

To start a new stripe, simply drop the old color at the edge and start working with the new color, leaving a tail.

After you've worked a few stitches, tie the two colors together at the edge of your work. Work to the end of the row and then back again.

When switching colors at the beginning of the row, always bring the new working color *under* the old color.

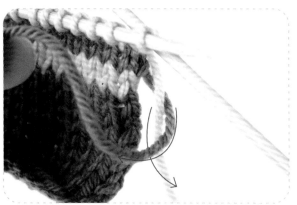

If your stripes are more than two rows tall, catch the old yarn at the edge by bringing the working yarn from *under* the old color.

To hide the yarn ends, use duplicate stitch weaving, following the matching color for each yarn end.

allover color:
stranded

Working more than one color across a row really isn't much more difficult than working with one color. The biggest challenge when color-knitting is dealing with the two strands of working yarn.

To work a pattern with frequent color changes, you carry all the colors needed for the row all the way across, "floating" the yarn across the back of the knitting when they're not being used. This is called *stranded*.

You work one stitch of stranded knitting at a time, right to left, just like plain knitting. It's usually worked in stockinette (stocking) stitch, and typically you use no more than two colors in one row. You carry both colors across the back as you knit so they're available for the next stitch.

Stranded color knitting is often referred to as *Fair Isle* knitting, after the traditional color knitting of the Fair Isle region.

This is what the back looks like:

The front looks like this:

Color knitting is usually represented in a chart. Each square in the chart represents one stitch. Here's an example of a chart with three colors: A, B, and C.

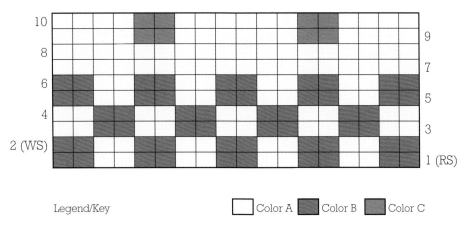

Legend/Key　　　　☐ Color A　▨ Color B　▨ Color C

Short Floats

The simplest stranded color knitting has small pattern repeats with short *floats*. The floats are the strands of yarn visible on the wrong side. Cast on 18 in Color A and work a few rows of stockinette (stocking) stitch, ending with a wrong side row.

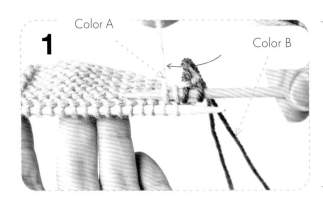

Color A

1

Color B

Drop Color A, pick up Color B, and knit 2 stitches. Now for the stranded part: drop Color B, bring color A *under* the dropped B yarn, and knit 2 stitches.

It doesn't matter which color goes over and which one under. Just try to be consistent to prevent the yarns from winding around each other. The yarn that travels under tends to be slightly dominant in the finished knitting.

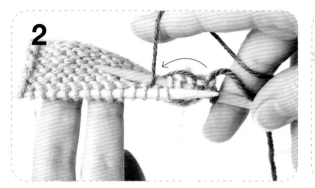

Drop Color A, bring Color B *over* the dropped A yarn, and knit 2 stitches. (At this point, tie the end of B with A at the edge to secure it.)

Continue alternating Colors A and B to the end of the row, bringing A *under* the dropped yarn and B *over* the dropped yarn.

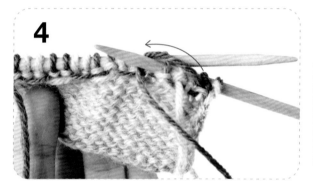

On the purl side, repeat the process, purling the stitches instead of knitting them. Remember, B goes *over* ...

... and A goes *under*.

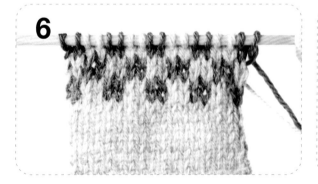

Work 4 more rows from the chart to make a small checkerboard pattern.

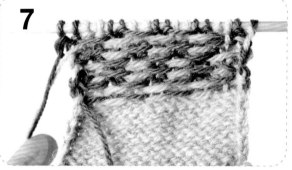

The back will look something like this.

Long Floats

If the floats between colors get longer than about 5 stitches, you need to weave them in. Work Rows 7 and 8 from the chart, and weave in on Row 9:

1

Work the first 9 stitches of Row 9. You're halfway through a 6-stitch span of Color A. Pick up B, lay it over your working yarn, and finish the row.

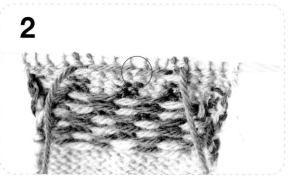

2

Here is the back, showing Color B woven in.

3

The idea is the same on the purl side. Halfway through Row 10, pick up B, lay it over the working yarn, and finish the row.

4

Here's the finished swatch. The surface isn't as smooth as with plain knitting, but blocking will fix most of that.

Carry the yarn across the back *loosely*. It takes some practice to maintain a perfect tension in stranded knitting. If your project combines plain knitting with stranded color work and the colorwork is tighter, use larger needles on the color sections.

---

blocks of color:
intarsia

If you're knitting blocks or sections of color, you can make color designs without carrying your yarn across the back. This is called *intarsia*, which comes from the Italian wood mosaic technique called *intarsio*. Intarsia is quite easy. You simply use a separate strand of color for each section and weave the colors together at the transition.

One thing to note about intarsia is that it doesn't work in the round; the yarn has to travel back and forth across the rows.

You need two colors of yarn, A and B. Cast on 17 stitches with Color A, and work a few rows of stockinette (stocking) stitch.

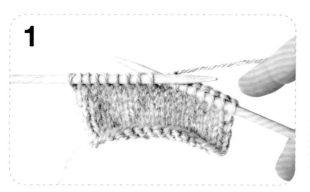

1

Knit 8 with A.

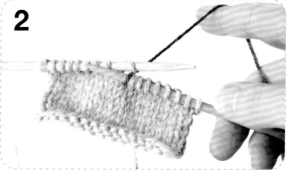

2

Now for a block of color: drop A, and start knitting with B. Let the yarn end of B hang down the back beside A.

3

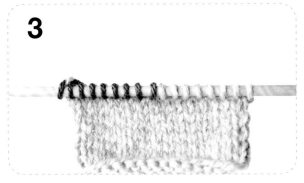

Knit to end with B.

4

On the wrong side, purl 9 in B. Then drop B, bring Color A from *under* B, and knit to the end with it.

5

That's really all there is to it! Every time you change colors, bring the working color from *under* the dropped color. This weaves the colors together along the edge of the color block.

You can use intarsia to work vertical or diagonal lines, weaving together the two colors on the back the same way.

cables and twisted stitches

twisting
stitches

Usually, if a stitch gets twisted accidentally, you correct it. However, you can intentionally twist a stitch for a textured effect. These twisted stitches look best in knit-purl combinations.

Let's compare regular stitches with twisted stitches. On the left, the two knitted columns of ribbing are worked normally, through the right, or front, leg of the stitch. On the right, the two knitted columns of ribbing are worked through the left, or back, leg of the stitch. In knitting instructions, this is called *through back loop* or abbreviated as *tbl*. Notice how the twisted stitches are more compact and look slightly braided.

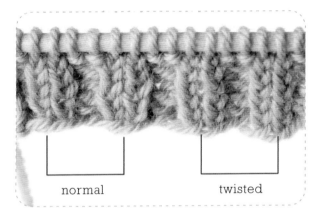

normal   twisted

1

To try working through the back loop, cast on 18 stitches. We're going to work a 2/2 rib, but with the first two columns twisted. Purl 2.

2

Put the needle tip through the back of the next stitch.

3

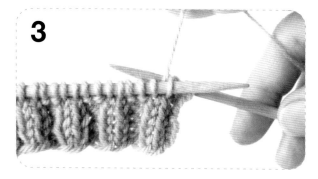

Wrap the yarn around your needle as you normally would to knit.

4

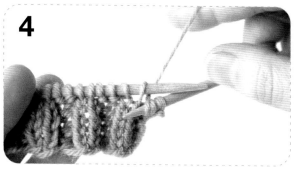

Pull the yarn through, and finish the row like this: knit the next stitch through back loop, purl 2, knit 2 through back loop, [purl 2, knit 2] twice, end with a purl 2.

5

Purling through back loop uses the same principle, but is a little awkward. Start the row like this: [knit 2, purl 2] twice, knit 2. Then put the needle to the left of the back loop.

6

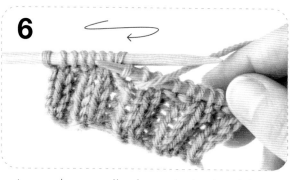

Insert the needle through the back loop, from left to right, and then back to the left and to the front of your work again. You'll see the back of the loop on the right needle.

7

Wrap the yarn around the needle as you normally would to purl, and purl the stitch. Finish the row like this: purl the next stitch through back loop, knit 2, purl 2 through back loop, [knit 2, purl 2] twice, end with knit 2.

cables

You knit cables by crossing columns of stitches, creating the illusion of a twisted rope. Cables are one of the most intriguing knitted textures, and the great news is, they're not that hard to make! Even an intricate cable is within the grasp of a beginner knitter.

To cross stitches when forming a cable's twist, you need an extra needle to hold the stitches that you need to temporarily set aside. This extra needle can be a double-pointed needle or a bent needle designed to stop the stitches from sliding off, called a *cable needle*. These needles come in different shapes and diameters. The cable needle's diameter doesn't have to match your needle's diameter, but try to use something close.

Let's try a 4-stitch *front-cross* cable. To start, cast on 12 stitches.

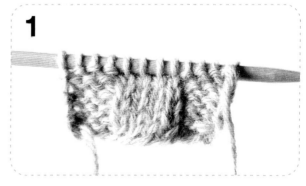

Work 5 rows to set up a column of 4 knits centered on a purled background, like this: Row 1 (wrong side): knit 4, purl 4, knit 4. Row 2: purl 4, knit 4, purl 4. Repeat these 2 rows for 3 more rows.

On the sixth row, purl the first 4 stitches. Take the yarn to the back so you're ready to knit the next stitch.

3

Slip the next 2 stitches (half of your column of 4 knits) onto a cable needle.

4

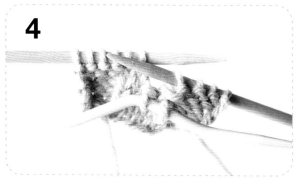

Let the cable needle hang at the front of your work.

5

Knit the next 2 stitches from the left needle.

6

Now knit the 2 stitches from the cable needle. You can let the left needle hang loose. Just be sure it doesn't drop any stitches.

7

Now purl to the end. See the twist?

8

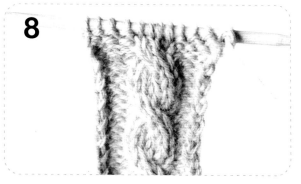

Repeat steps 1 through 7, continuing to work a front-cross every sixth row.

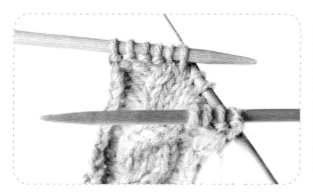

For a back-cross cable, let the cable needle hang at the back on step 4.

On the left is a basic *front-cross* cable; on the right is a *back-cross* cable.

That's it! With that simple twist, you can construct a wide variety of cables.

All four of the cables shown on the facing page use the same basic 4-stitch front-cross cable technique. You can create the different effects by changing the direction and frequency of the crosses and the number of stitches crossed. These variations are, from left to right:

- A *fancy 4-stitch cable* (work the front-crosses every fourth and tenth row)

- A *6-stitch wave cable* (alternate front-crosses and back-crosses)

- An *8-stitch horseshoe cable* (work a front-cross directly next to a back-cross)

- A *zigzag cable* (cross 2 knits over 1 purl).

making lace

lace
stitches

Knitted lace consists of clusters of holes on a stockinette (stocking) or garter stitch background and is noticeably open. It can look mind-bogglingly complex— and sometimes it is. But many lace patterns employ techniques you already know. The secret is in the arrangement of increases and decreases, and in the blocking.

All you need to know to knit basic lace is how to knit and purl, plus how to increase and decrease. By combining simple increases, like yarn overs, with decreases, like knit 2 together, you can knit lace.

Let's start with a simple lace pattern. Using a DK or fingering weight yarn, cast on 14 stitches, and purl 1 row. (I've worked a few rows already to make it easier for you to see.)

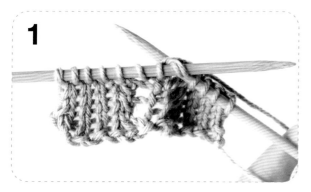

Knit 4 and then knit 2 together.

Yarn over. (Bring the yarn to the front and back over the right needle.)

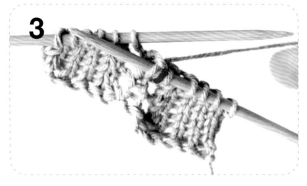

3

Knit 1. The yarn over creates a stitch.

4

Yarn over again.

5

Slip slip knit and then knit 4 to finish the row. Purl the wrong side rows, and repeat steps 1 through 5 on the right side rows.

If you repeat this simple idea—stacking increases and decreases—across some plain knitting, you get very attractive vertical columns of open stitches.

blocking
lace

Lace blocking isn't a big departure from what you already know. The goals in blocking lace are to flatten the knitting and to open up the stitches.

With lace blocking, you're opening the stitches and lightening the density of the knitted fabric more deliberately than with other knitting. With plain knitting, you don't want to stretch the stitches so far that you can see between them. But with lace, that's often exactly what you want, so all the components, including the connecting strands between stitches, are visible. There are more elaborate lace blocking techniques, but here's a basic method to get you started.

You need a couple large, clean towels; a large container or clean sink; a small amount of mild liquid detergent (specialty wool detergent is ideal, but a mild hand or dish soap works, too); and several rustproof pins.

How much to stretch?

How far you stretch out the lace depends on the looseness of the gauge (tension) and the yarn's weight and fiber. A loose gauge stretches more than a tight gauge, and fibers like silk and cotton may resist stretching while animal fibers like alpaca are relatively elastic. The key is to stretch the lace gradually until the knitting feels *slightly* taut against the pins but not so taut the yarn is weakened. When in doubt, stop stretching. You can always repeat the process to block out the knitting more, but it's difficult to undo blocking.

Before blocking, lace looks slightly scrunched and the surface is distorted. This fern lace swatch is a great example of why lace blocking is so important.

1

Fill a container with cool water, and dissolve in it a tiny amount of liquid detergent. Add the knitted fabric and let it soak until it's thoroughly saturated. Run cool water into the container until the water is clear (brightly colored yarns sometimes tint the water) and soap free.

2

Carefully lift the knitting from the container, supporting as much of it with your hands as you can. If the container is small enough, tip the water out first. Gently squeeze out as much water as you can by pressing—not wringing—the knitting.

3

Arrange two towels on your work area. Gently lay the knitting on the first towel, roll it up, and press down on the towel to squeeze out more water. Transfer the knitting to the second towel.

4

Pull the lace gently and gradually into shape, straightening the edges and opening the stitches. Pin at even intervals in several spots on all edges, pushing the pins in at a slight angle away from the knitting. You'll know you've stretched your knitting far enough when it's slightly taut against the pins.

knitting shorthand

"rep from *" and other
mysteries

Knitting instructions tend to be written in a condensed, specialized language. The primary reason for this is to save space on the page, but it also helps organize repeated steps for the knitter. You've probably noticed by now that knitting is quite repetitive!

This knitting shorthand can definitely be a hurdle to understanding patterns. Not every pattern writer or publisher uses the same shorthand, but here's a guide to some of the more commonly used conventions.

"Rep from *"

When you see an asterisk in knitting instructions, you know there's probably going to be a "rep from *" or "repeat from *" somewhere, too. The "rep from *" is a cue telling you to pause and scan back along the line to the last * and then work through the steps after the * again. Sometimes, the instructions follow the format of "rep from * *until*" or "rep from *, *ending with*." The *until* or *ending with* tells you the last repeat of the set will be slightly different. If you don't see any special instructions, keep repeating from the * until you run out of stitches. Otherwise, stop as instructed.

For example: The instruction says this:

> *Knit 2, purl 2; rep from * until 2 stitches remain; knit 2.

If you have 14 stitches, you would knit 2, purl 2, knit 2, purl 2, knit 2, purl 2, knit 2.

Parentheses ( )

Knitting instructions are littered with parentheses. They're used to separate sizes and to group steps.

Garment patterns are usually written for more than one size. Rather than write the instructions for each size individually, which would take a lot of room on the page, the instructions are written once, with the variations for each size separated by parentheses and commas.

For example: Let's say a sweater pattern can be made in five sizes: women's extra small, small, medium, large, or extra large. Instead of repeatedly writing that out throughout the pattern, the pattern might begin like this:

To fit women's sizes XS (S, M, L, XL)

The first size is followed by all the other sizes, separated by commas, enclosed in parentheses. In the pattern, any instructions where the numbers vary from size to size follow the same format:

Cast on 180 (190, 200, 210, 220) stitches.

So if you were making a size medium, you'd cast on 200 stitches.

Parentheses are also used to group multiple steps to clarify how they're worked.

For example: One way to increase 2 stitches is to knit 1, leave the stitch on the left needle, yarn over, and then knit 1 and slide the stitch off the left needle. But that's a very wordy way to explain it. Here's the knit-speak way:

(Knit 1, yarn over, knit 1) in 1 stitch

The parentheses are a cue that some steps are going to be grouped together.

Brackets [ ]

Square brackets are sometimes used, just like parentheses, to group steps. They're also used to explain how many times to repeat something.

For example: The instructions might say this:

[Knit 2, purl 2] 3 times, knit 2

This a shorter way of saying knit 2, purl 2, knit 2, purl 2, knit 2, purl 2, knit 2.

knitting
abbreviations

If you've looked at any knitting patterns, you probably noticed right away that patterns are full of abbreviations.

The abbreviations are another part of knit-speak and are primarily used to save space. But they're also very useful once you get used to them because they enable you to scan knitting instructions quickly.

You can become fluent in knitting abbreviations with just a little practice. But until then, do this: when you're starting a new pattern, read through it first. Whenever you encounter an abbreviation or a "rep from *" or a bracket, make a note in the margin or on a sticky note with the translation. This helps as you're knitting but also trains your knitter's brain. After you look up "k2tog" about three times, you'll never forget it means to knit 2 stitches together.

Abbreviations can also be combined. For example, you might see "slip 1 with yarn in back" written as *sl1 wyib,* or "purl 2 together through back loop" as *p2togtbl.*

Let's look at some commonly used abbreviations. Don't worry if you don't know what all these mean yet!

Abbreviation	Meaning	Abbreviation	Meaning
*	repeat the instructions following the * as directed	p, P	purl
		p2tog	purl 2 stitches together
(), []	work the instructions within parentheses or brackets as directed	p3tog	purl 3 stitches together
		pat, patt	pattern
alt	alternate, alternating	pm	place marker
approx	approximately	psso	pass slipped stitch over
beg	begin, beginning	pwise	purlwise
bet	between	rem	remain, remaining
BO	bind (cast) off	rep	repeat, repeating
C4B	cable 4 back	rev	reverse
C4F	cable 4 front	RH	right hand
CC	contrast color	rnd	round
circ	circular	RS	right side
cn	cable needle	sl	slip
CO	cast on	sl1-k2tog-psso	slip 1 stitch, knit 2 together, pass slipped stitch over
cont	continue, continuing	sl2-k1-p2sso	slip 2 as if to k2tog, k1, pass 2 slipped stitches over
dec, decr	decrease, decreasing		
dpn	double-pointed needle	sm	slip marker
foll	follow, following	ssk	slip, slip, knit 2 stitches together
inc, incr	increase, increasing		
k, K	knit	st(s)	stitch(es)
k2tog	knit 2 stitches together	st st	stockinette (stocking) stitch
k3tog	knit 3 stitches together	tbl	through back loop
kwise	knitwise	tog	together
LH	left hand	WS	wrong side
M1	make 1 stitch	wyib, wyb	with yarn in back
m1L	make 1 left-leaning stitch	wyif, wyf	with yarn in front
m1R	make 1 right-leaning stitch	yo	yarn over
MC	main color		

reading a knitting
chart

Instead of being written out as a pattern, knitting instructions are sometimes shown as symbols on a chart. A chart is a wonderfully logical and visual way to show the arrangement of stitches. Learning how to read a chart takes a little time, but it's worth it!

Common Chart Symbols

In a knitting chart, each stitch is represented by a small picture or symbol. Here are some commonly used symbols:

Knit on right side, purl on wrong side

Purl on right side, knit on wrong side

O Yarn over on right side

Knit 2 together on right side

Slip-slip-knit 2 together on right side

Knit (on right side), purl (on wrong side) through back of stitch

Slip 1, knit 2 together, pass stitch over on right side

Symbols can represent colors:

X In Color A, knit on RS, purl on WS

● In Color B, knit on RS, purl on WS

△ In Color C, knit on RS, purl on WS

Check the chart for which row numbers are for right side and wrong side:

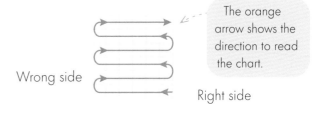

The orange arrow shows the direction to read the chart.

Wrong side

Right side

Reading a Pattern

A chart is shown from the right side of the knitting. Some charts use a square grid, and some, like this one, use a rectangular grid, because stitches are wider than they are tall.

Each square in the grid represents a stitch, and each horizontal line of squares represents a row of stitches. Each symbol tells you what stitch to work.

The vertical columns of numbers on the right and left show the row numbers. Usually (but not always!), odd numbers represent the right side rows.

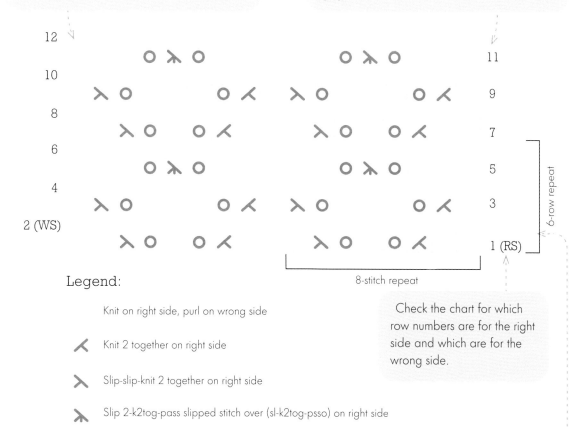

8-stitch repeat

6-row repeat

Legend:

Knit on right side, purl on wrong side

人 Knit 2 together on right side

入 Slip-slip-knit 2 together on right side

木 Slip 2-k2tog-pass slipped stitch over (sl-k2tog-psso) on right side

O Yarn over (yo) on right side (RS)

Check the chart for which row numbers are for the right side and which are for the wrong side.

The Legend, or Key, is essential to deciphering the chart. It tells you what each symbol means and how to work the stitch from the right and wrong side.

Many stitch patterns are repetitive. Brackets show you which steps are repeated, making it much easier for you to memorize the sequence of stitches. For easier patterns, look for repeats with small numbers, about 14 or smaller.

cable
charts and symbols

You're adept at reading knitting charts by now, but you might be wondering what *cables* look like on a chart. A cable symbol is a bit different from the usual knitting symbol because a cable is executed over multiple stitches. A charted cable is a great example of why knitting charts make visual sense—the cable symbol mimics the knitted cable very nicely and shows you which way the cable twists.

Common Cable Symbols

You'll find many variations of the knitted cable symbol, depending on the direction of the twist and how many stitches are involved. But the basic idea is always the same: the symbol shows how many stitches you put on the cable needle, whether they're held to the front or the back, and if they're knitted or purled:

Cables go by all sorts of names. You might see what I'm calling a cable 4 front called a 2/2 left cross, 4 front-cross, or a 2-over-2 front-cross. Don't try to learn all the styles. Just check the pattern's stitch guide or legend.

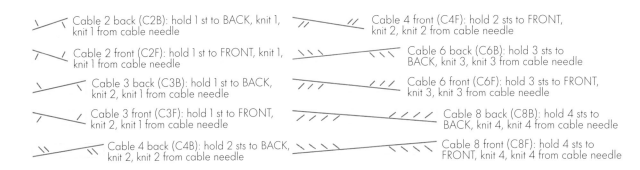

Cable 2 back (C2B): hold 1 st to BACK, knit 1, knit 1 from cable needle

Cable 2 front (C2F): hold 1 st to FRONT, knit 1, knit 1 from cable needle

Cable 3 back (C3B): hold 1 st to BACK, knit 2, knit 1 from cable needle

Cable 3 front (C3F): hold 1 st to FRONT, knit 2, knit 1 from cable needle

Cable 4 back (C4B): hold 2 sts to BACK, knit 2, knit 2 from cable needle

Cable 4 front (C4F): hold 2 sts to FRONT, knit 2, knit 2 from cable needle

Cable 6 back (C6B): hold 3 sts to BACK, knit 3, knit 3 from cable needle

Cable 6 front (C6F): hold 3 sts to FRONT, knit 3, knit 3 from cable needle

Cable 8 back (C8B): hold 4 sts to BACK, knit 4, knit 4 from cable needle

Cable 8 front (C8F): hold 4 sts to FRONT, knit 4, knit 4 from cable needle

Other Styles

Here are some style variations of cable symbols. These all mean cable 4 front.

Cable Chart

Now let's look at a full charted pattern of cables. (In fact, this is the charted version of the photo on the preceding spread.) Remember, when using a chart, always read through the legend or key first before taking a stitch.

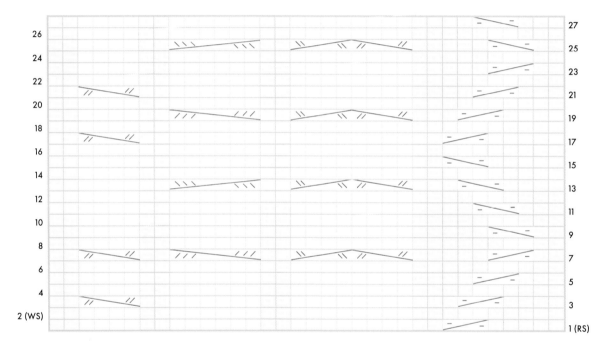

Legend/Key

☐ Knit on right side, purl on wrong side

☐ Purl on right side, knit on wrong side

 Cable 4 front: hold 2 sts to FRONT, knit 2, knit 2 from cable needle

Cable 4 back: hold 2 sts to BACK, knit 2, knit 2 from cable needle

Cable 6 front: hold 3 sts to FRONT, knit 3, knit 3 from cable needle

Cable 6 back: hold 3 sts to BACK, knit 3, knit 3 from cable needle

Twist 3 front: hold 1 st to FRONT, knit 2, purl 1 from cable needle

Twist 3 back: hold 1 st to BACK, knit 2, purl 1 from cable needle

more practice projects

felted
bowls

These fun little bowls are perfect for practicing circular knitting. If you make one in each size, they nest neatly together. Use them to hold keys, change, keepsakes, or small knitting supplies. As a bonus: the construction of these bowls is exactly the same as making a hat, so you're practicing for making hats here too— just in miniature.

Skills Needed

Working in the round, decreasing

Finished Measurements

About 2½ (3, 3½) inches (6.5, 7.5, 9cm) diameter, 1½ inches (4cm) high. Finished size depends on gauge and amount of felting.

Yarn

35 (45, 55) yards (32, 41, 50m) worsted weight wool, held double, or half that amount in bulky wool. Use feltable 100 percent animal fiber.
Don't use anything labeled as "superwash."
I used 100 percent Peruvian highland wool, and a blend of 70 percent Peruvian highland wool, 30 percent superfine alpaca.

Gauge (Tension)

15 stitches and 20 rows = 4 inches (10cm) in stockinette (stocking) stitch, before felting. Gauge (tension) isn't crucial for this project.

Needles

U.S. 10 (6mm/UK 4) needles for your preferred method for working in a small round

Other Supplies

Blunt yarn needle

Construction Notes

The bowls are worked from the top down and decreased for the base. After you bind off, you felt the bowls and block them to shape.

Held double means you knit with two strands held together and worked as one.

Felted Bowls

Cast on 24 (30, 36) stitches. Arrange for working in round, being careful not to twist your stitches.

Round 1: Knit all stitches.

Round 2: Purl all stitches.

Repeat Rounds 1 and 2 once more.

Next 6 (7, 8) rounds: Knit all stitches.

Large bowl only:

Next round (Dec): [K4, k2tog] 6 times—30 stitches.

Next round: Knit.

Medium and large bowls only:

Next round (Dec): [K3, k2tog] 6 times—24 stitches.

Next round: Knit.

All sizes:

Next round (Dec): [K2, k2tog] 6 times—18 stitches.

Next round: Knit.

Next round (Dec): [K1, k2tog] 6 times—12 stitches.

Next round (Dec): [K2tog] 6 times—6 stitches.

Cut the yarn, thread the tail onto the blunt yarn needle, and thread through the remaining 6 stitches, removing them from your needles. Pull the tail tight, and weave in the ends.

Felting

The easiest way to felt the bowls is in the washing machine: put the bowls in a mesh laundry bag or closed pillowcase and add them to your next hot-water load. Or you can felt by hand: put the bowls in a clean sink with hot water and a little bit of dish detergent, and agitate for 15 to 30 minutes. Then mold each damp bowl over the base of a glass or can, and let dry.

Your bowl starts like this:

Comes out of the wash looking like this:

And ends up like this after blocking!

leafy
ornaments

In this project, you use increasing and decreasing to shape your knitting into a leaf. These charming leaves are perfect as embellishments on gift wrapping, as hanging ornaments, or as gifts all on their own. They're quick to make and use very little yarn, so you can make a whole pile of leaves in no time!

Finished Measurements

Each leaf is about 2 inches wide by 3 inches tall (5cm wide by 7.5cm tall) after blocking.

Yarn

Each leaf uses 6 yards (5.5m) medium (worsted, aran) weight yarn. I used 100 percent wool, and a blend of 80 percent baby alpaca, 20 percent acrylic.

Gauge (Tension)

18 stitches and 26 rows = 4 inches (10cm) in stockinette (stocking) stitch. Gauge (tension) isn't crucial for this project.

Needles

U.S. 7 (4.5mm/UK 7) straight or circular needles

Other Supplies

Blunt yarn needle

Construction Notes

The leaf is worked from the stem to the tip.

Leafy Ornaments

Cast on 3 stitches, leaving a long tail.

Odd-numbered rows are right side.

Rows 1 and 2: Knit across.

Row 3 (Increase [Inc]): Knit 1, yarn over (yo), knit 1, yarn over (yo), knit 1—2 increased, 5 stitches on needle.

Row 4: Knit 2, purl 1, knit 2.

Row 5 (Inc): K2, yo, k1, yo, k2—2 increased, 7 stitches.

Row 6: K2, p3, k2.

Row 7 (Inc): K3, yo, k1, yo, k3—2 increased, 9 stitches.

Rows 8, 10, 12, 14: K2, p5, k2.

Rows 9, 11, 13: Knit across.

Row 15 (Decrease [Dec]): K2, slip-slip-knit 2 together (ssk), k1, knit 2 together (k2tog), k2—2 decreased, 7 stitches.

Row 16: Repeat Row 6.

Row 17 (Dec): K2, slip 2-knit 1-pass 2 over (sl2-k1-p2sso), k2—2 decreased, 5 stitches.

Row 18: Repeat Row 4.

Row 19 (Dec): K1, sl2-k1-p2sso, k1—2 decreased, 3 stitches.

Row 20: Knit across.

Row 21 (Dec): Sl2-k1-p2sso—2 decreased, 1 stitch.

Cut your yarn. Loosen the stitch on the needle, and slide it off. Thread the tail through the stitch, and pull closed.

Finishing

Block as desired. The more water you use to block, the flatter the leaf.

Weave in the tail at the tip of the leaf. Use the tail at the stem end to hang the leaf, or weave it in if you prefer.

mini
pincushions

These adorable pincushions are a great way to practice your colorwork—and use up leftover bits of yarn. All your yarn ends are hidden on the inside, and your stitch tension isn't crucial. I've included two versions here: the Checker Pincushion, which is done in intarsia, and the Diamond Pincushion, which uses stranded knitting.

Skills Needed

Stranded and intarsia color knitting, blanket stitch for seaming edges

Finished Measurements

About 2½ inches (6.5cm) square

Yarn

Worsted weight yarn in the following amounts: about 20 yards (18m) Main Color, plus about 4 yards (3.5m) each in Colors A, B, C, D, E (for the Checker Pincushion) or 10 yards (9m) Color B (for the Diamond Pincushion). I used 100 percent superwash merino and 100 percent wool.

Gauge (Tension)

20 stitches and 27 rows = 4 inches (10cm) in stockinette (stocking) stitch. Gauge (tension) isn't crucial for this project, but you don't want to knit too loosely or the stuffing will show through your stitches.

Needles

U.S. 5 (3.75mm/UK 9) straight or circular needles

Other Supplies

Blunt yarn needle, stuffing to fill your pincushion (available at fabric or craft supply stores)

Construction Notes

You knit the pincushion in a rectangle, fold it in half, stitch around the edges, and stuff it.

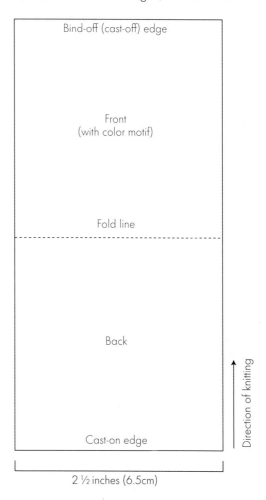

Mini Pincushions

With Main Color, cast on 13 stitches.

Row 1 (Right Side): Knit across.

Row 2: Knit 1, purl to last stitch, knit 1.

Rows 3 through 15: Repeat the pattern established in Rows 1 and 2.

Row 16: Knit across. (This is the fold line.)

For the Checker Pincushion: Work all rows from the chart, using intarsia for the contrast colors.

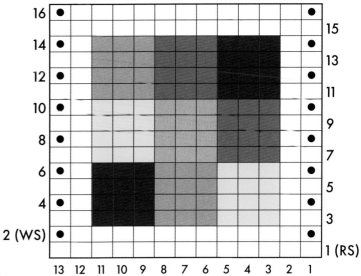

Legend/Key

☐ Main Color: Knit on RS, purl on WS

⬜• Main Color: Knit on WS, purl on RS

▦ Color A: Knit on RS, purl on WS

⬛ Color B: Knit on RS, purl on WS

☐ Color C: Knit on RS, purl on WS

▨ Color D: Knit on RS, purl on WS

▩ Color E: Knit on RS, purl on WS

For the Diamond Pincushion: Work all rows from the chart, using stranded knitting for the contrast color.

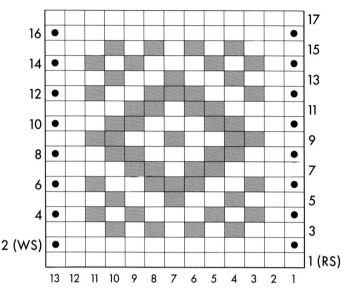

Legend/Key

☐ Main Color: Knit on RS, purl on WS

⊡ Main Color: Knit on WS, purl on RS

▦ Color A: Knit on RS, purl on WS

Finishing

Bind (cast) off, leaving a tail about 24 inches (61cm) long. Weave in all tails except the long tail on the wrong side. Thread the long tail onto the blunt yarn needle. Fold the fabric at the fold line, with the wrong sides together, to form a square. Blanket stitch around three edges of the square, including the folded edge, fill with stuffing, and blanket stitch the fourth edge closed. Moisten and block the pincushion to shape it.

lace
bookmarks

Sure, you can practice lace patterns by making a swatch, but why not turn that swatch into something useful, like a knitted bookmark? This project gets you used to "reading" your lace stitches and working from a chart, and it also shows you two traditional types of lace construction. It's all in the balance and position of increases and decreases.

Skills Needed

Foundation lace stitches

Finished Measurements

About 1 ¼ inches (3cm) wide by 6½ inches (16.5cm) tall

Yarn

About 20 yards (18m) fingering weight yarn per bookmark. I used 75 percent superwash merino and 25 percent nylon.

Gauge (Tension)

25 stitches and 33 rows = 4 inches (10cm) in lace, blocked. Gauge (tension) isn't crucial for this project.

Needles

U.S. 3 (3.25mm/10 UK) straight or circular needles

Other Supplies

Blunt yarn needle

Lace Bookmarks

Cast on 13 stitches.

First row (WS): K1, purl 11, k1.

Work from Chevron Lace or Shetland Leaves chart.

For the Chevron Lace Bookmark:

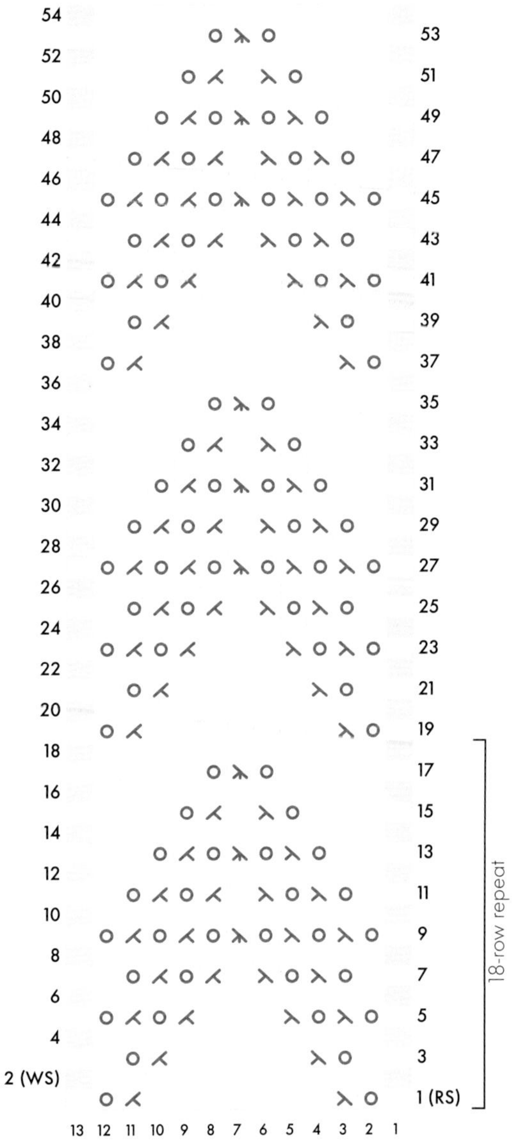

Legend/Key

Knit on RS, purl on WS

Purl on RS, knit on WS

Knit 2 together

Slip-slip-knit 2 together

Slip 1-knit 2 together-pass stitch over

Yarn over

For the Shetland Leaves Bookmark:

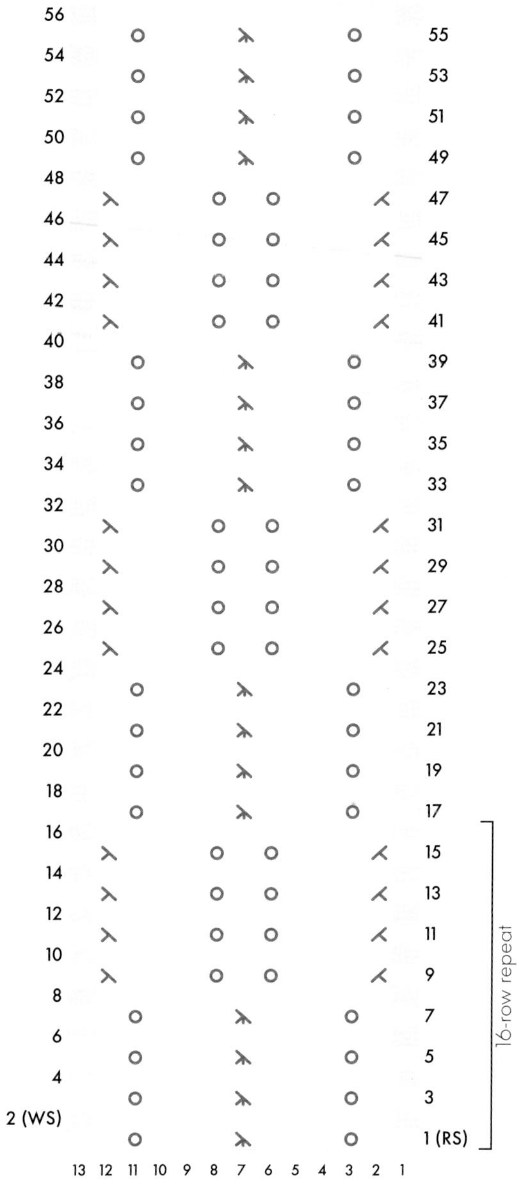

Legend/Key

Knit on RS, purl on WS

Purl on RS, knit on WS

Knit 2 together

Slip-slip-knit 2 together

Slip 1-knit 2 together-pass stitch over

Finishing

Bind (cast) off. Lace block the bookmark. Be patient and thorough when blocking, and pin the edges at several spots. Accentuate the point at the bottom edge of the Shetland Leaves pattern when blocking if you like. Weave in the ends.

The chevron pattern lies relatively flat because the yarn overs are directly next to the decreases and the left-leaning slip-slip-knits are balanced by the right-leaning knit-2-togethers. The Shetland leaves lace puckers and scallops dramatically. This is caused by the distance between the yarn overs and the decreases and also by staggering the groups of decreases every eight rows. After you've knitted the bookmarks, don't skip the blocking. Lace really comes to life in the blocking process.

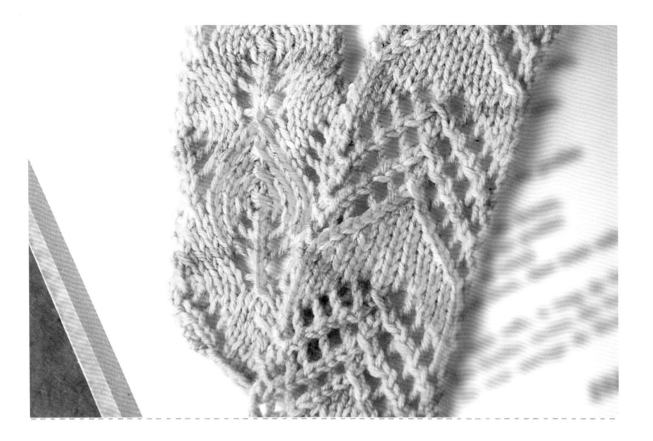

tips and tricks

knitting from patterns

finding the right
pattern

Knitting patterns are widely and easily available. Check out the knitting section in your local library or bookstore, and you're sure to find some pattern books. Your newsstand likely stocks knitting magazines, and these always contain several brand-new patterns. And of course, the internet is a fantastic resource for patterns. Let's look at some things you should consider when picking a pattern.

Fit

Find a pattern that gives you the size you need, for the fit you want. Trying to make a pattern bigger or smaller as you go by changing stitches or yarn thickness is a bit like trying to get a square peg into a round hole.

For a garment, the pattern should tell you the finished measurements (the chest circumference is usually the defining measurement) and often, the amount of *ease*. Ease is the difference between the person's measurements and the garment's. If ease is specified in a pattern, it can tell you a lot about how the garment is meant to fit. For example, 0-inch (0cm) ease is very fitted, whereas 4-inch (10cm) or more ease is loose and oversized.

Not sure what kind of ease or fit you like in a sweater? The best thing to do is measure a sweater or shirt you like wearing. Lay the sweater or shirt flat, and measure the chest, hips, length, and sleeve length. These key dimensions will help you when choosing a pattern.

To determine your preferred amount of ease, measure your own chest circumference, and subtract it from that of the sweater or shirt you like wearing.

Skill Level

Most—but not all—patterns provide general information about the skills required. This is sometimes indicated with a difficulty category, for example, Beginner or Intermediate. Other patterns will use a scale, for example, 1 out of 4 being easy and 4 out of 4 being the most advanced.

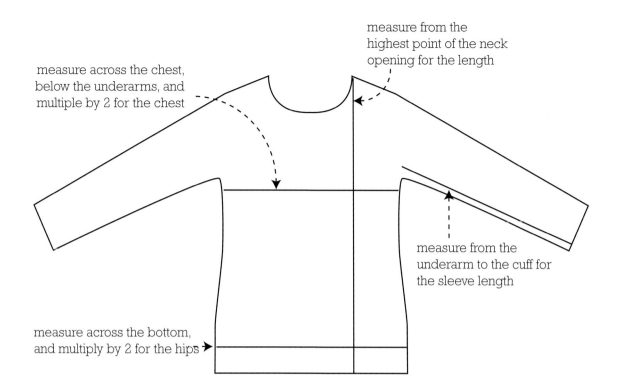

measure from the highest point of the neck opening for the length

measure across the chest, below the underarms, and multiple by 2 for the chest

measure from the underarm to the cuff for the sleeve length

measure across the bottom, and multiply by 2 for the hips

Complexity

If you want a simple pattern, avoid things that add complexity. Complexity often comes with details. Pockets, multiple textures, colorwork, seams, and belts all make a pattern more complex.

Yarn Choice

Choose a pattern that's suitable for the yarn you want to knit with. For example, if you're happiest working with midweight yarn, like worsted or DK, don't commit to a cardigan worked in fine or very bulky yarn.

Commitment

It's easy to get inspired by impressive patterns, but finishing something big can be difficult even for experienced knitters. Don't be afraid to challenge yourself, but do avoid overcommitting. An incomplete project or a false start can be discouraging. You'll get a lot of satisfaction by successfully completing a few small projects before trying out something big.

reading a
pattern

The shorthand used in knitting instructions goes beyond abbreviations and parentheses; it even shapes how patterns are organized on the page. Knitting patterns have dozens, or even hundreds of steps, often in a limited amount of space. So knitting designers and publishers use abbreviations and shorthand, but they also arrange and format patterns using common conventions. Reading a knitting pattern is a little bit like reading a recipe in a cookbook. With a little experience, you'll learn where information should be on the page and be able to find it quickly.

The best way to read a pattern is to simply *read* it. It's all too easy to get excited about a new project and cast on without looking ahead. Take a few minutes to read a pattern from the beginning to the end. Make a note of any materials you'll need as well as any terms or techniques you're not familiar with.

When you're reading through the pattern, take extra care when looking at the following key sections.

Gauge (Tension)

In any project that has to fit, such as clothing, gauge (tension) is absolutely essential.

Yarn Requirements

Be sure you have enough yarn in the right weight to complete the whole project.

Needles

Check that you have all the needle sizes and types required.

Notions or Other Supplies

This section tells you if you need things like buttons, cable needles, or a crochet hook.

Size, Fit, and Schematics

The pattern should include information on the finished size or sizes, as well as a drawing with detailed dimensions, called a schematic.

Technical or Construction Notes

Pay special attention to this section. These notes tell you important aspects of how the project goes together. It also gives you a clue how complex the pattern is.

Stitch Guide

This section usually explains any abbreviations used in the pattern.

Special Techniques

It's always good to check for this section; it can be a clue that the pattern has some complexity.

Charts

Look through any charts and their legends before beginning.

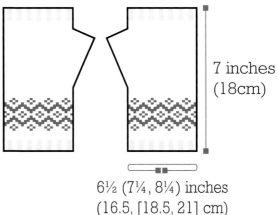

7 inches
(18cm)

6½ (7¼, 8¼) inches
(16.5, [18.5, 21] cm)

expert finishing

IN THIS CHAPTER

blocking

Let's dive a little deeper into blocking. The larger and more complex your knitting gets, the more attention you'll want to pay to blocking. Blocking helps you get the exact finished measurements and shows your knitting and yarn at its best.

When you're deciding on which blocking method to use, take care to first read the yarn label. It might contain specific notes. Also, it's sometimes worth blocking a test swatch before blocking your whole project.

To block, you'll need an iron with a steam setting, two clean dry towels, a mild liquid detergent, a large container or clean sink, and several rustproof pins.

Steam Blocking

Blocking with steam loosens the knitting, allowing you to shape it, and the heat sets the stitches in their pinned position without putting any physical pressure on the knitting.

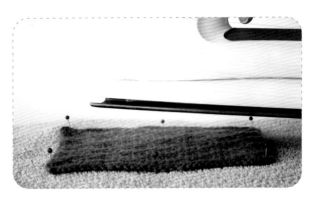

Pin your piece to a thick towel. Hold your iron set to its highest steam setting *above* but not touching your knitting. Allow the steam to permeate all areas of the knitting. If desired, you can gently shape and re-pin your knitting.

Use caution with steam. It might be too extreme for some fibers. And it goes without saying that steam is *very* hot, so please take care not to burn yourself.

Water Blocking

Wet-blocking is the most thorough way to block your knitting, although it has a long drying time. Take care when getting animal fiber wet. Any agitation can cause some wet animal fiber to felt.

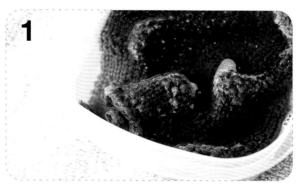

Soak your knitting in cool water with a little mild detergent. Run cool, clean water into the container to rinse.

Lift out the knitting carefully. Squeeze—but don't wring—out excess water.

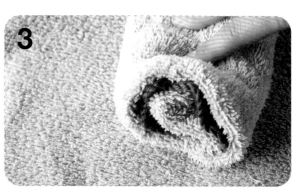

Roll your knitting in a clean, dry towel, and press gently to remove excess water.

Arrange the damp knitting on a second dry towel, and gently nudge it into shape, using a ruler to straighten the edges.

Pin the knitting and allow it to dry.

sewing

Most knitting projects involve some sewing. The sewing can sometimes be one of the most noticeable aspects of a knitted item, so it's worth taking a little time to do it carefully.

When joining knitted pieces together, use the same yarn you used to knit the pieces, unless the yarn is very thick. In that case, use a thinner yarn in a matching color. You'll also need a blunt yarn needle, sharp scissors, and some safety pins.

Mattress Stitch

The mattress stitch is frequently used to sew knitted pieces together because it makes a strong and nearly invisible join, but it does have some bulk to it. How you do the mattress stitch depends on whether you're joining stitches to stitches, rows to rows, or rows to stitches.

Sewing Stitches to Stitches

You might use this method for joining a shoulder seam.

1
Line up your two pieces to be joined with the right sides up. Insert the needle from back to front through the rightmost stitch on one piece, and pull through, leaving a tail.

2
Thread the needle, from the front, under two halves of one stitch on the adjoining piece. Pull the yarn through so the knitted pieces touch, but don't pull tight yet.

3

Thread the needle under the next two stitch halves on the first piece, starting where the yarn came out. Again, don't pull the yarn tight.

4

Continue threading through two stitch halves at a time, on alternate sides of the seam, until you've worked about 2 inches (5cm) of the seam.

5

Gently pull the yarn tight.

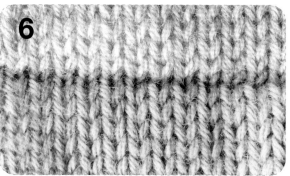

6

Repeat until you've finished joining.

Before you sew any seam, line up the knitted pieces to be joined along the entire length of the join. If you want, use safety pins to loosely hold the pieces in place.

Sewing Rows to Rows

This mattress stitch method is used, for example, to join side seams. Again, start with your knitted pieces right sides up.

If joining a side seam, start by securing the yarn at the base: bring the needle from the back, between the 2 leftmost stitches on the right-hand piece, and then from the back between the 2 rightmost stitches on the left-hand piece. Then repeat, bringing your yarn up through the same spot on each side. Pull tight.

Take a look between the columns of stitches, and you'll see horizontal strands there, 1 strand for every row. Thread the needle from the front under the bottommost 2 of these strands and pull the yarn through, but not tightly.

Do the same thing on the left-hand piece, catching 2 strands.

Work your way up, back and forth, catching the next 2 strands each time, until you've worked about 2 inches (5cm) of the seam.

Gently pull the yarn tight.

Work your way up the seam, tightening every 2 inches (5cm) until you've finished joining.

Sewing Stitches to Rows

You sometimes have to join pieces perpendicular to each other, like when joining a sleeve to an armhole. In this case, simply combine the rows-to-rows and stitches-to-stitches methods.

Thread the needle under 2 stitch halves on one piece and under 2 row strands on the other.

Because you'll have more rows than stitches in this kind of join, every fourth time or so, pick up 3 strands instead of 2.

Should you block before or after sewing? There's no set rule, but blocking before makes the process much easier, and the pieces line up better.

Whip Stitch

A mattress stitch, although nice looking from the right side, is quite bulky. If you need something with less bulk, you can make a flat seam using a whip stitch. This seam is visible, and it's not as strong as mattress stitch, so reserve it for side seams, stitching very short seams, or attaching pocket linings. You work a whip stitch the same whether you're joining rows or stitches.

Arrange the pieces with the wrong sides up. Thread the needle through half of a stitch on one piece and through half of a stitch on the adjoining piece. Pull the yarn through but not tight.

Skip a stitch and repeat step 1. You'll work every second stitch of knitting.

Continue, tightening the yarn every few stitches, until your seam is complete.

From the right side, a whip stitch seam is slightly visible.

Blanket Stitch

Blanket stitch is a decorative stitch that's worked from the outside. It adds a finishing touch to the edge of a piece of knitting or felted fabric. You can work blanket stitch from the right or the wrong side.

1

Thread the needle through the stitch at rightmost edge of your work, from front to back. Pull through, leaving a tail. Thread the needle through again from the front, a little to the left. As you bring the needle through, bring it *over* the working yarn. On the first stitch, be sure the tail is *under* the working yarn.

2

Continue working to the left, taking the needle through from the front and *over* the working yarn. As you pull the yarn through, be sure the loop of each sewn stitch lies at the very edge of the knitting.

3

Blanket stitch looks the same from the front ...

When you sew knitted pieces together, don't pierce the yarn.

4

... as it does from the back.

picking up
stitches

Sometimes you'll want to add knitting to a piece that's already bound (cast) off. For example, you might add a collar to a sweater, a pocket to a jacket, or an arm to a stuffed critter. Instead of casting on a separate piece and then sewing it on, you can use existing stitches as your foundation row. This technique is called *picking up stitches.*

Picking Up Stitches from Stitches

You can pick up and knit from a bound (cast) off edge of stitches—at the back of a neckline, for example.

1

Have the right side of your knitting facing you, and start at the right-hand edge of where you want to add stitches. Insert your needle into the center of the first stitch.

2

Wrap your yarn around the needle as if to knit.

3

With the needle tip, pull the yarn through to the front.

4

Proceed leftward, picking up and knitting through each stitch.

Picking Up Stitches from Rows

You pick up stitches from the ends of rows when you add knitting to the vertical edge of a piece of knitting—if you wanted to add a button band to a cardigan, for example.

Have the right side of your knitting facing you, and start at the right-hand edge where you want to add knitting. Insert your needle 1 stitch in from the edge, *between* 2 stitches closest to the edge. (For less bulk, pick up from the *center* of the edge stitch.)

Wrap your yarn around the needle as if to knit.

With the needle tip, pull the yarn through to the front.

Continue leftward, picking up and knitting between columns. To compensate for the difference in gauge (tension) between the rows and the picked-up stitches, don't pick up a stitch for every row. A good general rule is to skip every fourth row.

Picking Up Stitches on the Face of Your Knitting

If you want to add a pocket, for example, you might pick up stitches from the front of a sweater.

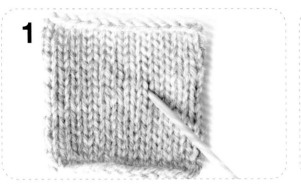

Have the right side of the work facing you. Starting at the rightmost edge where you want to add knitting, insert the needle into the center of a stitch.

Lift up the head, or top, of the stitch, pulling it to the front. Wrap your yarn around the needle as if to knit.

Pull the yarn through the head of the stitch so you have a stitch on the needle.

Proceed to the left, picking up and knitting 1 stitch onto the needle for every stitch on the face of the knitting.

sewing on
buttons

One of my favorite parts of finishing is choosing buttons. There's such a fun variety of buttons available, with handmade and vintage options, too.

You'll need buttons, a blunt yarn needle, matching yarn, scissors, and safety pins.

Before you begin, check that your needle fits through the button's holes.

This might sound obvious, but be sure the button fits through the button hole, too.

Lay your knitting flat on a table, and mark the locations for your buttons with safety pins. Pay special attention to lining up stripes, pockets, and necklines.

Thread your needle through the marked spot from front to back and then back to front, leaving a tail.

Place your button on the marked and stitched spot, and bring the needle up through the back of the button and down through the other hole through the knitted fabric. Secure the button by repeating this step once or twice. The heavier the button, the more it needs to be secured.

Bring the needle from back of your knitting to the front, but not through the button. You'll come out underneath the button.

Cut the yarn.

Tie the tails together twice, snugly.

Snip the ends so they're just hidden by the button.

i-cord

An I-cord is a knitted tube. It looks fussy to make, but it isn't. Elizabeth Zimmermann "unvented" this technique and dubbed it "idiot cord" because of the technique's simplicity.

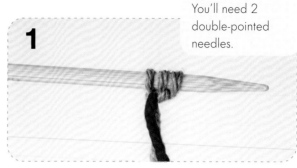

You'll need 2 double-pointed needles.

Cast on 3 to 5 stitches. Arrange the stitches so the working yarn is at the *left* edge of the cast-on (instead of the right where it would normally be), and put the needle with the cast-on in your left hand.

Pull the working yarn across the back on the first stitch, and knit across.

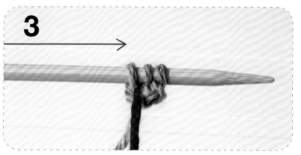

At the end of the row, put the needle with the stitches back in your left hand, but again, keep the working yarn at the left edge of the knitting. Slide the stitches to the right tip of the needle.

Repeat steps 2 and 3 until your I-cord is the desired length. The yarn is carried across the back and concealed inside the tube.

Pull gently on the bottom of the tube to tighten it. Bind (cast) off normally.

weaving

1

You'll need a blunt needle.

On the wrong side, locate the path of the yarn on the row where the yarn end is. The yarn winds up and down underneath purl bumps, and you'll follow that path with your needle. Thread your yarn end onto a blunt needle, and insert it up and under the first 2 purl bumps.

Sometimes, you need to weave in the ends more discretely, either because the ends are in the middle of a row or they are visible. You can camouflage a yarn end on the back of your knitting using *duplicate stitch*.

A duplicate stitch follows the path of existing stitches and blends in. When using duplicate stitch to hide yarn ends, weave them in on a matching color. I'm using a contrasting color here to make the method more visible.

2

Thread the needle back down under the next 2 purl bumps, still following the yarn path.

3

Continue following the yarn path for about 3 or 4 more stitches.

4

Snip the ends close to the knitting.

trouble-shooting

dropped
stitches

The Freshly Dropped Stitch

When a knitter gasps in the middle of a row, it's probably because of a freshly dropped stitch. Don't panic, but do deal with it right away.

Dropped stitches fall into three categories: a *freshly dropped stitch* you quickly need to pick back up, a *laddered drop stitch* several rows down that needs a little knitting "surgery" to repair, and the *unfixable dropped stitch* that can't be picked up but can be anchored and hidden.

For any kind of dropped stitch, if you're not immediately sure how to fix it, put a crochet hook or cable needle through it to stop it from unraveling until you decide what to do. An unchecked dropped stitch can unravel all the way to your cast-on edge.

Fix a dropped stitch immediately, before it creates a problem.

With the tip of whichever needle the stitch dropped from, pick up the stitch, keeping the right "leg" of the stitch on the top.

The Laddered Drop Stitch

If a dropped stitch continues to unravel, you end up with more than one dropped stitch in a vertical column called a ladder. You can tell if you have a ladder if you see horizontal strands that used to be stitches that look like rungs of a ladder.

Fixing a dropped stitch with one ladder is pretty easy.

Pick up the dropped stitch, front to back, with the right leg of the stitch on the front.

Pick up the strand, from front to back.

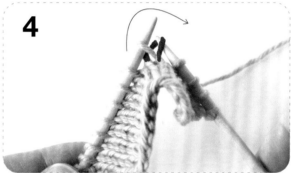

Lift the dropped stitch over the strand and off the needle.

Drop a purl stitch? It's a little easier to fix dropped stitches from the knit side, so flip your work over, fix the drop, and flip your work back over.

1

A larger ladder is trickier to fix, but it uses the same technique as the short ladder. You'll need a crochet hook.

2

With the right side facing you, insert the crochet hook through the dropped stitch from front to back. Gently pull the knitting to the left and right of the drop to reveal the ladder of strands.

3

Hook the lower rung on the ladder ...

4

... and pull it through the first stitch.

5

Keep moving up the ladder, hooking each rung through in order. Slip the final stitch off the crochet hook and on to your needle.

The Unfixable Dropped Stitch

Sometimes a stitch will drop and go unnoticed. And now, it's lying there, waiting to unravel and ruin your knitting. If the dropped stitch is too far down to pick up, or you've already bound (cast) off, you can secure and hide the stitch if it's in a discrete spot. You'll need to use a matching yarn to fix the dropped stitch; I'm using a contrasting color for the photos.

Put a cable needle through the dropped stitch. (Dropped stitches tend to pop forward on the knit side.)

Thread a blunt yarn needle with a piece of matching yarn, and from the wrong side, catch the top of the stitch with your yarn needle.

Pull the yarn through until the stitch is at the middle of the yarn. Remove the cable needle, and weave in both ends of your yarn.

The secured stitch viewed from the right side isn't completely invisible, but much better than it was!

If securing and hiding the stitch doesn't work—for example, if it's in a prominent spot—you might have to unravel back to the dropped stitch and rework your knitting.

fixing a
stitch

If you knit when you should have purled or purled when you should have knit, it's not a major problem. Fixing a stitch is totally doable, and when done carefully, it won't be noticeable.

Fixing a stitch in stockinette (stocking) stitch isn't very difficult if you have a crochet hook.

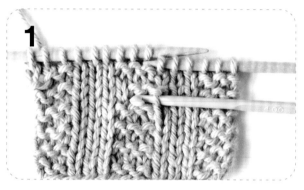

From the front, put a crochet hook through the center and under the left leg of the incorrect stitch.

Arrange the stitches on your needles on either side of the column that contains the incorrect stitch. Drop the top stitch at the top of the column and pull out all the stitches down to the crochet hook.

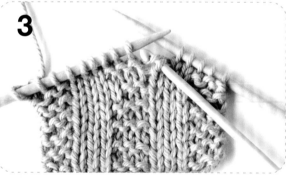

Starting at the bottom rung of the ladder, use the crochet hook to pull each rung through the stitch on the hook until you reach the top.

Fixing a mix of knits and purls is a little trickier but follows the same principle. You need to be able to read your knitting to do this.

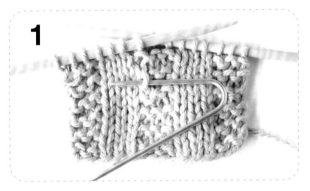

1

From the front, put a cable needle through the stitch directly *below* the incorrect stitch.

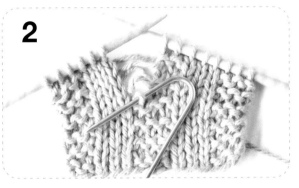

2

Arrange your needles on either side of the problem column and ladder down to the cable needle.

3

From the back, put the crochet hook through the center of the stitch on the cable needle. Remove the cable needle.

4

Hook the first rung of the ladder.

5

Pull the rung through the stitch on the hook. This creates a purl stitch.

6

Put the cable needle through the stitch on the crochet hook, and remove the hook.

7

Fix the next stitch from the front.

Here, the 4-rung ladder needs to be repaired in a column of garter stitch. So fix the next ladder from the back to purl, and the following from the front to knit.

wrong stitch
count

Knitting requires a lot of counting. Patterns usually alert you to changes in the stitch count as you go along, but counting the stitches on your needles and not getting the same number the pattern says should be there can be frustrating.

If your stitch count is off by 1 or 2 stitches, don't panic. If you have too many stitches, compensate with k2togs in discrete spots. If you have too few stitches, work some m1Ls. No one will notice.

If you're off by a lot of stitches, it could be a problem. Count your stitches again, and read through the pattern carefully. If you see where you went wrong, you can rewind to where you made the mistake and start again.

If you need to unwind a lot or all of your work, wrap the yarn around a piece of cardboard as you unravel it. Remove the loop of yarn from the cardboard, and tie it in at least two spots with contrasting yarn. Soak the loop in cool water until the kinks relax. Carefully remove the yarn from the water, taking care to keep the loop intact. Blot it on a clean, dry towel, and let it dry.

Pulling Out Stitches

If you have to undo your work, you can go back a little or a lot. Let's start by undoing a row or two a stitch at time.

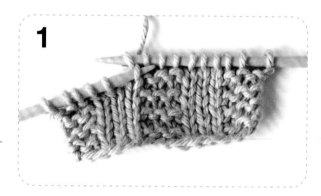

With the working yarn on your right needle, put your left needle under the right leg of the stitch *below* the first stitch on the right needle.

2

Pull the first stitch off the right needle.

3

Pull the working yarn free from the stitch.

If you have several rows of knitting to undo, working one stitch at a time would take a while. It's time to undo several rows.

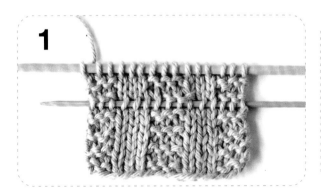

1

Lay your work flat, and thread a knitting needle under the right leg of each stitch in the row you want to unravel to. If you can, use a thinner needle than you used to work the piece.

2

Remove your working needle, and unravel the yarn down to the second needle.

common
mistakes
and how to avoid them

Mistakes can happen. But they don't have to. Let's look at some common mistakes new (and experienced!) knitters make and learn how to avoid them.

Count (Everything) (Twice)

This simple advice can save a lot of heartache. After you cast on, count and re-count your stitches. Spot check once in a while, too. You can catch dropped stitches or accidental increases right away if your stitch count changes when it shouldn't. Also, count your stitches when you're shaping a piece. The shaping sections of patterns are often the most complex and easy to make mistakes in.

Measure Carefully

When you measure, it's often a key part of a garment, like sleeve length or body width. Smooth your work flat on a table to measure, and measure from as many points as you can. It's better to catch a too-short sleeve or too-narrow body sooner rather than later.

Look at It in the Light

It's best to work in a well-lit spot so you can see any dropped stitches or split yarn. And every once in a while, hold up your work to the light. Light shining through the back of knitting can highlight gaps in the yarn and dropped stitches.

Holding your work up to the light reveals split strands like this one.

Blocking

Most, if not all, patterns end with the instruction to *block*. This step comes at the end, but it's not an optional afterthought. If you want to get the best texture and the best fit, follow the blocking instructions.

Check Your Gauge (Tension)

It's too easy to gloss over this step. Gauge (tension) doesn't *always* matter. Scarves, blankets, and washcloths can come out the wrong size, and they're still usable. But the dimensions of a sweater, hat, or mitt matter.

You should block your gauge (tension) swatch, too. All fibers will do something when you get them wet, and some change dramatically. Superwash fibers, very fine animal fibers, rayon, and cotton are all notorious for stretching, swelling, or shrinking.

Also be aware of your own knitting tension. Do you knit tighter in the round? Looser in ribbing? Make any necessary adjustments if so.

Twisted Join

One of the most frustrating—and easy to make—mistakes all knitters make at some point is twisting the cast-on edge when joining to work in the round. There's no good solution to this problem, except the heartbreak of undoing all your work. Check for twists when you join, double-check two or three rounds in, and then triple-check 10 rounds in.

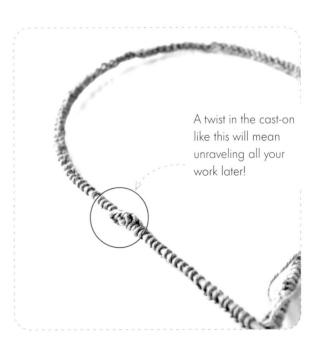

A twist in the cast-on like this will mean unraveling all your work later!

a gallery of knitting stitches

basic stitch
gallery

Stitch patterns are recipes for knitted textures. Just like the stitch patterns earlier in the book, these combine knits and purls. You choose how many to cast on. And although you can use any yarn you like, something smooth helps show off the subtle textures the stitches create.

I start out using plain English in the instructions and ease in to using abbreviated knit-speak. Practice a few of these stitch patterns, and you'll soon be fluent.

Knit 2/Purl 2 Ribbing

You learned a knit 1/purl 1 ribbing earlier. Now we're going to change it just a little bit and make a knit 2/purl 2 ribbing. Working it is a lot like the knit 1/purl 1, but it looks quite different. A 1/1 ribbing is rather fluffy, while the 2/2 is tighter and the ribs are more pronounced. A 2/2 ribbing looks the same on both sides, and it doesn't curl, making it great for borders and scarves.

Cast on a multiple of 4, plus 2, stitches. For example, cast on 26 (4 × 6 = 24 + 2 = 26).

Row 1: Knit 2, *purl 2, knit 2; repeat from * to end of row.

Row 2: Purl 2, *knit 2, purl 2; repeat from * to end of row.

Repeat Rows 1 and 2.

You'll notice the vertical columns emerging after just a few rows.

Seed (Moss) Stitch

Seed (moss) stitch is one of the prettiest textures in knitting, and it's so easy to do. It's also called Irish moss stitch, and you might even see it called "hailstones" in a traditional fishermen's sweater. You alternate single knits and purls to make a flat, highly textured, dense fabric that's the same on both sides. Seed (moss) stitch is great for almost anything and can be used as an allover texture or in small sections.

Cast on an odd number of stitches.

All rows: Knit 1, *purl 1, knit 1; repeat from * to end of row.

See how you're always alternating knits and purls? If you're ever wondering what comes next, just remember to alternate. If you just worked a purl, it's time to knit. Another way to check: if the next stitch was a purl bump on the previous row, knit it.

Garter Stitch Welt

A *welt* in knitting is a raised stripe or band. A garter stitch welt is an easy way to make stripes with very little extra work, alternating a few rows of stockinette (stocking) stitch with a few rows of garter stitch. When you get the hang of it, you can invent your own welt patterns!

Cast on any number of stitches. (Odd-numbered rows are right side rows, even-numbered rows are wrong side rows.)

Rows 1 through 6: Knit all stitches.

And now a 5-row band of stockinette (stocking) stitch:

Rows 7 and 9: Knit.

Rows 8 and 10: Purl.

Rows 11 and 12: Knit.

Finish off with 2 rows of stockinette (stocking) stitch:

Row 13: Knit.

Row 14: Purl.

Repeat Rows 1 through 14.

Box Stitch

A popular texture, the box stitch (also called double seed stitch and sometimes double moss stitch) is similar to seed (moss) stitch, but instead of alternating single knits and purls, you alternate little 2 × 2 squares of knits and purls. This makes a great all-purpose texture that's the same on both sides.

Cast on a multiple of 4, plus 2, stitches. For example, cast on 26 (4 × 6 = 24 + 2 = 26).

Row 1: Knit 2, *purl 2, knit 2; repeat from * to end of row.

Row 2: Purl 2, *knit 2, purl 2; repeat from * to end of row. (You'll notice the first two rows start like knit 2/purl 2 ribbing.)

Row 3: Now, purl every knit stitch and knit every purl stitch. That is, p2, *k2, p2; rep from * to end. (See how I snuck in some abbreviations there?)

Row 4: K2, *p2, k2; rep from * to end.

Repeat Rows 1 through 4.

Broken Rib

In a conventional rib, you alternate vertical columns of knits and purls. In a broken rib, you substitute a texture like garter stitch or seed (moss) stitch for the purl columns. The resulting texture isn't as stretchy as conventional ribbing, but it looks a lot like it. It lies quite flat and is lovely on both sides.

Cast on a multiple of 6, plus 3, stitches. For example, cast on 27 (6 × 4 = 24 + 3 = 27).

Row 1 (Right Side): Purl 3, *knit 3, purl 3, repeat from * to end of row.

Row 2 (Wrong Side): Purl all stitches.

Repeat Rows 1 and 2.

After a few rows, you'll see vertical columns against a background of garter stitch.

Variation: A garter stitch broken rib works nicely in almost any configuration. For example, try a 1/1 ribbing, but purl all the even-numbered rows.

Wave Stitch

You can arrange purls into almost any shape, as the wave stitch demonstrates. It's deeply textured with a bit of bounce.

Cast on a multiple of 14 stitches. For example, cast on 28 (14 × 2 = 28).

Row 1 (Right Side): Purl 2, *knit 10, purl 4; repeat from *, but end the last repeat with purl 2 instead of purl 4.

Row 2 (Wrong Side): Knit 3, *purl 8, knit 6; repeat from *, but end last repeat with knit 3 instead of knit 6.

Row 3: K2, *p2, k6, p2, k4; rep from *, end last rep k2 instead of k4.

Row 4: P3, *k2, p4, k2, p6; rep from *, end last rep p3 instead of p6.

Row 5: K4, *p6, k8; rep from *, end last rep k4 instead of k8.

Row 6: P5, *k4, p10; rep from *, end last rep p5 instead of p10.

Repeat Rows 1 through 6.

Basket Weave Stitch

Basket weave stitch patterns look like woven strips. They also show how, when mixed together, knits and purls come forward or recede. Vertically, knits look raised, like in a ribbing. Horizontally, purls look raised, like in a garter stitch welt.

Cast on a multiple of 10, plus 1. For example, cast on 21 (10 × 2 = 20 + 1 = 21).

Row 1 (Right Side): Knit all stitches.

Rows 2 and 4 (Wrong Side): Purl 2, *knit 7, purl 3; repeat from *, but end the last repeat purl 2 instead of purl 3.

Row 3: K2, *p7, k3; rep from *, end last rep k2 instead of k3.

Row 5: Knit.

Rows 6 and 8: K4, *p3, k7; rep from *, end last rep k4 instead of k7.

Row 7: P4, *k3, p7; rep from *, end last rep p4 instead of p7.

Repeat Rows 1 through 8.

Seed (Moss) Block

You can pair seed (moss) stitch, one of the most versatile knitted textures, with plain stockinette (stocking) stitch in many ways. Here, a checkerboard of plain blocks and seed (moss) blocks makes a very attractive texture.

Cast on a multiple of 10, plus 5, stitches. For example, cast on 35 (10 × 3 = 30 + 5 = 35).

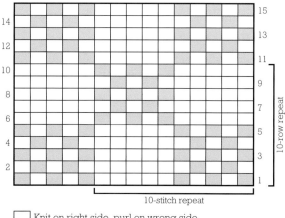

☐ Knit on right side, purl on wrong side
▨ Purl on right side, knit on wrong side

Seeded Chevron

Like seed (moss) block, seeded chevron combines seed (moss) stitch with plain knitting for a handsome texture. You'll find many variations of Seeded Chevron; this is one of the simpler ones. It's ideal for scarves and hats and for adding texture to sweaters.

Cast on a multiple of 8, plus 1, stitches. For example, cast on 25 (8 × 3 = 24 + 1 = 25).

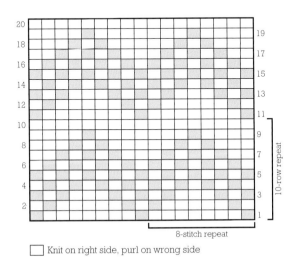

10-row repeat

8-stitch repeat

☐ Knit on right side, purl on wrong side
☐ Purl on right side, knit on wrong side

Large Diamond

Geometric motifs with strong diagonals work well in knitted textures. Here, you make a large diamond motif by surrounding plain knitting with moss (double moss) stitch. This pattern is lovely on both sides, so it's great anytime you need a reversible fabric, as with scarves.

Cast on a multiple of 14, plus 1, stitches. For example, cast on 29 (14 × 2 = 28 + 1 = 29).

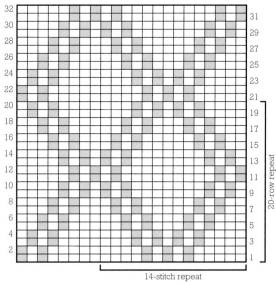

14-stitch repeat

20-row repeat

☐ Knit on right side, purl on wrong side
▨ Purl on right side, knit on wrong side

Diagonal Rib

Stagger a standard ribbing pattern every 2 rows, and you get a very attractive diagonal texture. This is a great pattern for scarves because it doesn't curl and it's reversible.

Cast on a multiple of 6, plus 3, stitches. For example, cast on 27 (6 × 4 = 24 + 3 = 27).

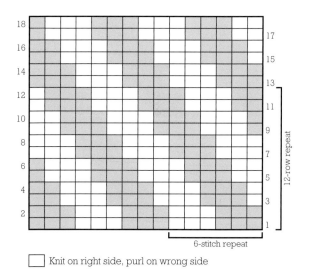

6-stitch repeat

12-row repeat

☐ Knit on right side, purl on wrong side
▨ Purl on right side, knit on wrong side

Twisted Rib Check

Twisted stitches make a tight and sharply textured fabric. Here, you alter a twisted rib by breaking it up into blocks. The result is a nicely understated fabric.

Cast on a multiple of 8, plus 3, stitches. For example, cast on 27 (8 × 3 = 24 + 3 = 27).

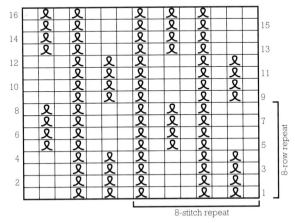

Knit on right side, purl on wrong side

Knit tbl on right side, purl tbl on wrong side

Simple Eyelet

This is an easy way to turn a yarn over into an allover stitch pattern. Simply scatter single eyelets across plain stockinette (stocking) stitch.

Cast on a multiple of 6, plus 3, stitches. For example, cast on 27 (6 × 4 = 24 + 3 = 27).

Small Eyelet Diamonds

Sometimes called quatrefoil, lace diamonds, or openwork diamonds, this is a lovely arrangement of eyelets, grouped in small diamonds. Here, the decreases are all slanted to the right, making the diamonds quite pronounced.

Cast on a multiple of 8, plus 1, stitches. For example, cast on 25 (8 × 3 = 24 + 1 = 25).

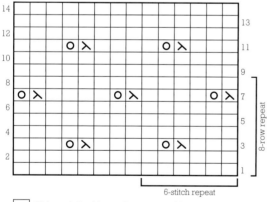

☐ Knit on right side, purl on wrong side

⟋ Knit 2 together on right side

◯ Yarn over on right side

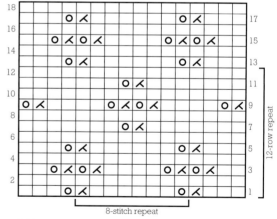

☐ Knit on right side, purl on wrong side

⟋ Knit 2 together on right side

◯ Yarn over on right side

Shetland Waves

Traditional Shetland stitch patterns are passed down through generations. One frequently used Shetland lace motif alternates clusters of yarn overs with clusters of decreases to create a graceful but easy-to-work wave pattern.

Cast on a multiple of 11 stitches. For example, cast on 33 (11 × 3 = 33).

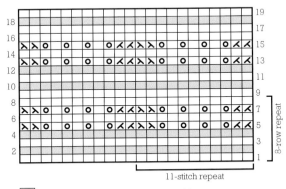

Knit on right side, purl on wrong side

Purl on right side, knit on wrong side

Yarn over on right side

Knit 2 together on right side

Slip-slip-knit 2 together on right side

Lace Ladder

When yarn overs are stacked vertically like this, the horizontal strands created by the yarn overs look like rungs on a ladder. This lace ladder makes an open mesh that's lovely for lightweight summer scarves.

Cast on a multiple of 6, plus 1, stitches. For example, cast on 31 (6 × 5 = 30 + 1 = 31).

Lace Arrows

You could use this pretty little lace pattern as a border or an allover motif. The decreases on either side of the "arrows" form a lovely subtle texture.

Cast on a multiple of 6, plus 1, stitches. For example, cast on 31 (6 × 5 = 30 + 1 = 31).

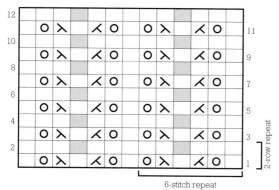

Knit on right side, purl on wrong side

Purl on right side, knit on wrong side

Knit 2 together on right side

Slip-slip-knit 2 together on right side

Yarn over (yo) on right side

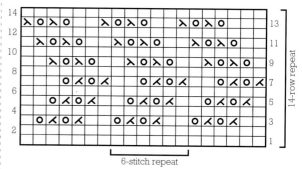

Knit on right side, purl on wrong side

Yarn over (yo) on right side (RS)

Knit 2 together on right side

Slip-slip-knit on right side

Vine Lace

One of my personal favorites, this vine lace, often called "traveling" vine lace, has a very simple foundation. Alternated pairs of yarn overs and decreases make a vinelike texture with a slightly scalloped edge.

Cast on a multiple of 9, plus 4, stitches. For example, cast on 31 (9 × 3 = 27 + 4 = 31).

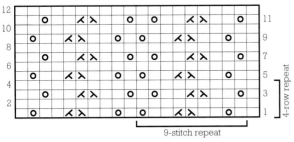

□ Knit on right side, purl on wrong side
⊙ Yarn over (yo) on right side (RS)
☒ Knit 2 together on right side
☒ Slip-slip-knit 2 together on right side

Lace and Cable Panel

Don't forget you can mix and match different kinds of knitting! Take a simple lace motif like this chevron lace panel, for example, alternate it with a basic 4-stitch cable, and you get a lovely fabric that would make a pretty scarf or panel on a sweater.

Cast on a multiple of 17, plus 8, stitches. For example, cast on 25 (17 × 1 = 17 + 8 = 25).

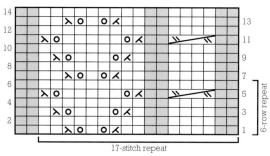

Knit on RS, purl on WS
Purl on RS, knit on WS
Yarn over on RS
Knit 2 together on RS
Slip-slip-knit 2 together on RS
Cable 4 back: slip 2 sts to cable needle, hold in back, knit 2, knit 2 from cable needle

Aran Cable Stitch

A traditional allover cable pattern, frequently seen on Aran sweaters, this is done by knitting 4-stitch cables next to each other instead of separating them, making a honeycomb texture. The gauge (tension) in this kind of cable work tends to be very compressed.

Cast on a multiple of 8 stitches. For example, cast on 32 (8 × 4 = 32).

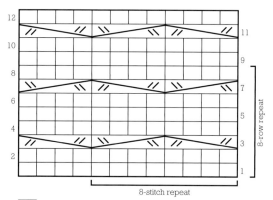

Knit on RS, purl on WS
Cable 4 back: slip 2 sts to cable needle, hold in back, knit 2, knit 2 from cable needle
Cable 4 front: slip 2 sts to cable needle, hold in front, knit 2, knit 2 from cable needle

Fern Lace

This traditional lace pattern creates a beautiful diamond leaf motif. On Row 7, note that a k2tog is used on the right edge and an ssk on the left.

Cast on a multiple of 10, plus 1, stitches. For example, cast on 31 (10 × 3 = 30 + 1 = 31).

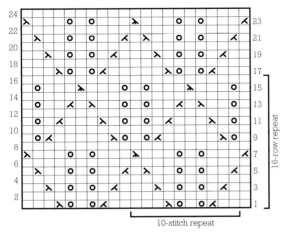

10-stitch repeat

16-row repeat

☐ Knit on right side, purl on wrong side
🝡 Slip 1-knit 2 together-pass stitch over
🅾 Yarn over (yo) on right side
🝠 Knit 2 together on right side
🝢 Slip-slip-knit 2 together on right side

Twisted Rib Cable

This unusual cable pattern is worked over an odd number of stitches. By working through the back of the ribs, you get a deeply textured and dense fabric. When you follow the steps for the cable shown on the legend, notice you're knitting into previously purled stitches and vice versa.

Cast on a multiple of 9, plus 2, stitches. For example, cast on 29 (9 × 3 = 27 + 2 = 29).

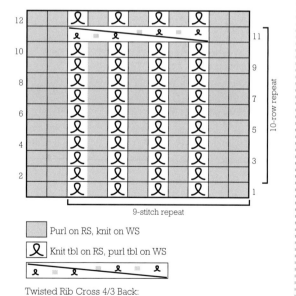

Purl on RS, knit on WS

Knit tbl on RS, purl tbl on WS

Twisted Rib Cross 4/3 Back:
Slip 3 to cn, hold at front, k1tbl, p1, k1tbl, p1,
[K1tbl, p1, k1tbl] from cn

Hearts

This sweet pattern would make a lovely border on a little girl's sweater. Or try it in a subdued, grown-up color combination for an allover pattern on an adult's hat.

Cast on a multiple of 10, plus 1, stitches. For example, cast on 31 (10 × 3 = 30 + 1 = 31). For an allover pattern, repeat Rows 2 through 15.

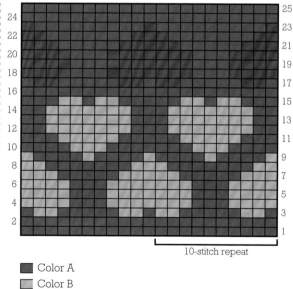

Color A
Color B
Color C

Braided Cable

A braided, or plaited, cable is easy to make by staggering front- and back-cross cables. This cable looks great in a hat or scarf or running up the front of a sweater.

Cast on a multiple of 9, plus 3, stitches. For example, cast on 30 (9 × 3 = 27 + 3 = 30).

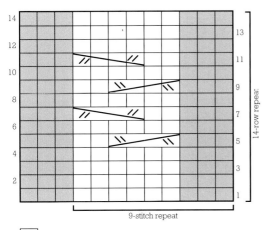

Knit on RS, purl on WS

Purl on RS, Knit on WS

Cable 4 back: slip 2 sts to cable needle, hold in back, knit 2, knit 2 from cable needle

Cable 4 front: slip 2 sts to cable needle, hold in front, knit 2, knit 2 from cable needle

Fair Isle

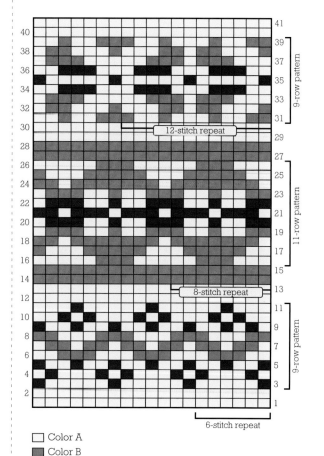

Fair Isle knitting refers to the stranded color knitting from the Shetland Islands. Characterized by kaleidoscope-like patterns and shifting colors, Fair Isle knitting usually combines several motifs in one garment.

These designs use typical Fair Isle shapes: small diamonds, zigzags, X's and O's. Although only 2 colors are used in a row, Fair Isle often changes both background and foreground colors frequently, creating a spectrum effect. These three motifs are a little simpler, with only the foreground color changing.

Cast on using the pattern multiple (6, 8, or 12), plus 1, stitches.

☐ Color A
▨ Color B
■ Color C

Ski Sweater

This color chart is inspired by the geometric designs and crisp color palette of traditional Scandinavian knitting. Change the color combination for a completely different look!

Cast on a multiple of 18, plus 1, stitches. For example, cast on 37 (18 × 2 = 36 + 1 = 37). To frame the pattern nicely, work one plain row of Color A and then start with Row 2 of the chart.

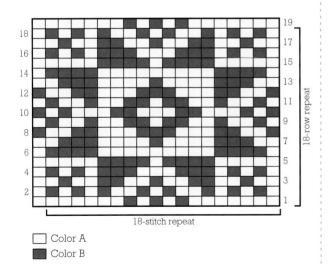

18-stitch repeat

18-row repeat

☐ Color A
■ Color B

a gallery of patterns

spa
towel

● ○ ○ ○ ○

Take full advantage of the
prettiness of seed (moss)
stitch with this simple hand
towel. This is a straightforward
project that combines texture
with plain knitting. A couple of
these towels—paired with a
few Garter Stitch Washcloths,
perhaps—make a lovely
house-warming gift.

Skills Needed

Combining knits and purls

Finished Measurements

About 10 inches (25.5cm) wide by 15 inches (38cm) long

Yarn

1 ball double-knit (DK) weight yarn, 50 grams/123 yards (112m). I used Knit Picks CotLin, 70 percent cotton, 30 percent linen.

Gauge (Tension)

20 stitches and 28 rows = 4 inches (10cm) in stockinette (stocking) stitch, after blocking. Gauge (tension) isn't crucial for this project.

Needles

U.S. 5 (3.75 mm/UK 9) straight needles

Other Supplies

Blunt yarn needle

- -

Changing the size of your towel is easy. To make it wider, increase your cast-on, being sure to use an odd number of stitches. To make it longer, work more repeats of stockinette (stocking) and seed (moss) stitch bands.

- -

Spa Towel

Cast on 51 stitches.

Work 18 rows of seed (moss) stitch: Knit 1, *purl 1, knit 1; repeat from * to end.

Then work 3 rows of stockinette (stocking) stitch:

Next row (Right Side): Knit all stitches.

Next row (Wrong Side): Purl all stitches.

Next row: Knit all stitches.

Follow it with 3 rows of seed (moss) stitch: Knit 1, *purl 1, knit 1; repeat from * to end.

Repeat the last 6 rows 10 more times. To change the length, work more or fewer repeats.

Work 3 rows of stockinette (stocking) stitch.

Finish with 18 rows of seed (moss) stitch.

Bind (cast) off.

Finishing

Block your towel, and weave in the yarn ends.

buttoned
phone case

With this project, you can protect your phone with a knitted phone case, and practice your finishing skills at the same time! This also is a fun excuse to use a couple cute buttons. You can easily adapt this basic pouch for other delicate items, like glasses.

For a fun challenge, you could knit this case in the round. Then the only seam would be at the base.

Skills Needed

Yarn over and knit 2 together, mattress stitch, sewing buttons

Finished Measurements

6¼ × 3¼ inches (16 × 8.25cm). This case fits a phone that's 5½ × 2¾ inches (14 × 7cm).

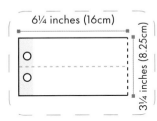

Yarn

1 ball fine weight (sport or light DK) yarn, 50 grams/131 yards (120m) per ball. I used Knit Picks Galileo, 50 percent merino, 50 percent viscose from bamboo.

Gauge (Tension)

22 stitches and 32 rows = 4 inches (10cm) in stockinette (stocking) stitch, after blocking

Needles

U.S. 5 (3.75mm/UK 9) straight needles

Other Supplies

Blunt yarn needle, 2 small buttons

Construction Notes

The case is worked flat and then joined at the back and the base.

Buttoned Phone Case

Cast on 38 stitches.

Work in stockinette (stocking) stitch, knitting right side and purling wrong side rows, until your knitting measures 5½ inches (14cm).

Work 4 rows in garter stitch, knitting every row.

Next row (RS) (buttonhole row): Knit 15, yo, k2tog, k5, yo, k2tog, knit to end.

Work 4 more rows in garter stitch. Bind (cast) off.

Finishing

Block piece. After blocking, fold the rectangle with wrong sides together and join the back seam. Center the back seam, and join the bottom of the pouch. Sew on the buttons to match the buttonhole position.

intarsia messenger
bag

● ● ● ● ○

This fun and trendy bag is
easy to knit and assemble and
makes a great excuse to
practice your intarsia skills.
The felting process results in
a firm, sturdy fabric, and a
small inner pocket makes this
a very practical accessory.
Follow the chevron motif on
the flap like the bag in the
picture, or invent your own
intarsia motif!

Skills Needed

Intarsia colorwork, felting, basic sewing

Finished Measurements

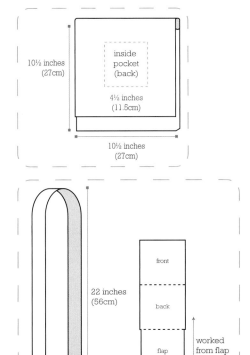

inside pocket (back)

10½ inches (27cm)

4½ inches (11.5cm)

10½ inches (27cm)

22 inches (56cm)

front

back

flap

worked from flap up

Bag: 10½ inches (27cm) wide by 10½ inches (27cm) tall

Strap: 22 inches (56cm) from halfway point

Final measurements will vary depending on how much you felt the fabric.

Yarn

250 grams/275 yards (251m) bulky (chunky) yarn: 200 grams/220 yards (201m) Main Color (MC) plus 25 grams/28 yards (25m) each Colors A and B. Use feltable 100 percent animal fiber. Don't use anything labeled superwash. I used a Peruvian Highland wool and alpaca blend.

Gauge (Tension)

12 stitches and 18 rows = 4 inches (10cm) in stockinette (stocking) stitch before felting. Gauge (tension) isn't crucial for this project, but looser stitches will help the felting process.

Needles

U.S. 11 (8mm/UK 0) straight needles

Other Supplies

Blunt yarn needle

Matching thread and sharp needle for stitching

Construction Notes

The bag is worked flat in one piece, from the flap up. The motif on the flap is worked using intarsia. The strap and pocket are worked separately. Join the bag's side seams and then block all the pieces. Sew on the strap and pocket after felting.

Intarsia Messenger Bag

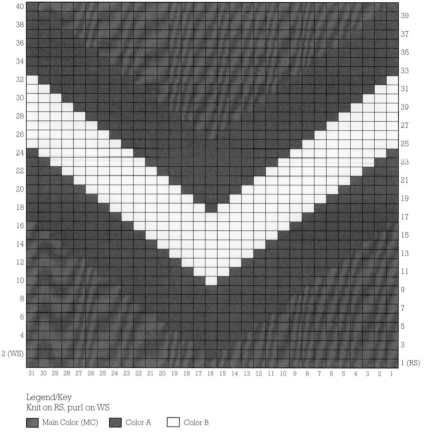

Legend/Key
Knit on RS, purl on WS

■ Main Color (MC)   ▨ Color A   ☐ Color B

Flap

With MC, cast on 31 stitches.

Purl 1 row.

Work 40 rows from chart.

Continue in MC for the remainder of bag.

Work 4 rows, knitting RS and purling WS.

Back

Next row (RS; Inc): Kfb, knit to last stitch, kfb—33 stitches.

Work 44 rows, knitting RS and purling WS.

Base

Knit 5 rows, starting and ending with WS.

Front

Work 45 rows, knitting RS and purling WS.

Bind (cast) off.

Pocket

With MC, cast on 15 stitches.

Work 18 rows, knitting RS and purling WS.

Bind (cast) off.

Strap

With MC, cast on 115 stitches.

Knit 2 rows.

With A, knit 2 rows.

With B, knit 2 rows.

With MC, knit 2 rows.

With MC, bind (cast) off.

Finishing

Fold the bag at the base with wrong sides facing and, using MC and mattress stitch, join sides, starting at the top of the garter stitch base. Then whip stitch the bottom corners across the garter stitch base.

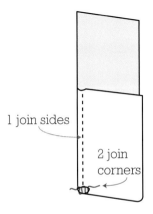

1 join sides

2 join corners

Weave in all ends.

Turn the bag inside out, and felt all pieces.

Block all the pieces right side out, shaping them carefully, and allow to dry.

With matching thread or yarn, sew the strap to the wrong side of the top side edge. Center the pocket to the wrong side of the back 1 inch (2.5cm) from the top of the bag, and sew on.

- - - - - - - - - - - - - - - - - - - -

Here are a few more intarsia ideas. Or create your own design! Make it bold so it won't be obscured by the felting.

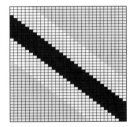

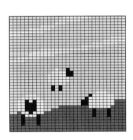

chunky textured
cowl

● ○ ○ ○ ○

A quick-knit neck warmer for cold weather, this cowl is a great beginner project. It's as satisfying to finish as a scarf, but with far less knitting. The moss (double moss) stitch texture lies flat and is easy to memorize. When you're finished knitting, dress up this cowl with your favorite buttons.

Traditional knitted textures often have more than one name. "Moss" stitch in the United States is "double moss" stitch in the UK, while the UK's "moss" stitch is "seed" stitch in the United States, which means you also might see this stitch called "double seed" stitch!

Skills Needed

Knit-purl combinations, yarn overs, sewing buttons

Finished Measurements

9 inches (23cm) high and 20 inches (51cm) around, buttoned

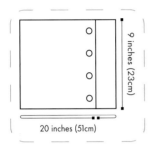

Yarn

1 skein bulky (chunky, 12-ply) yarn, 100 grams/ 110 yards (100m) per skein. I used a superwash merino wool and nylon blend.

Gauge (Tension)

12 stitches and 16 rows = 4 inches (10cm) in moss (double moss) stitch

Needles

U.S. 10.5 (6.5mm/UK 3) straight needles

Other Supplies

Blunt yarn needle, 4 medium buttons, matching finer yarn or embroidery floss for sewing buttons

Construction Notes

This cowl is knit flat in a rectangle with easy yarn over buttonholes along one end and buttoned closed.

Chunky Textured Cowl

Cast on 27 stitches.

Work in moss (double moss) stitch as follows, or follow the chart:

(The stitch pattern is reversible, so no "right" or "wrong" side is noted.)

Row 1: Knit 1, *purl 1, knit 1; repeat from *.

Row 2: Purl 1, *knit 1, purl 1; repeat from *.

Row 3: Purl 1, *knit 1, purl 1; repeat from *.

Row 4: Knit 1, *purl 1, knit 1; repeat from *.

Repeat Rows 1 through 4 22 more times.

Next row (buttonholes): Knit 1, purl 1, knit 1, *yarn over, k2tog, [purl 1, knit 1] 2 times; repeat from * to end.

Repeat Rows 2 through 4.

Bind (cast) off.

Finishing

Block and weave in ends. Fold the rectangle shut with the buttonhole end overlapping the nonbuttonhole end by ¾ inch (2cm). Sew on the buttons using a matching, finer yarn or embroidery floss, lining up the buttons with the buttonholes.

branching eyelet
scarf

● ● ○ ○ ○

With a little garter stitch and a few strategically placed eyelets, you can knit a fabric that looks quite ornate. This pretty little scarf is meant to give you the most bang for your knitting buck, with plenty of plain knitting and a small, easily memorized pattern repeat.

Skills Needed

Casting on, combining knits and purls, yarn overs, knit 2 together (k2tog), slip-slip-knit (ssk)

Finished Measurements

About 6½ inches (16.5cm) wide by 60 inches (1.5m) long

Yarn

3 balls fine weight (sport or light DK) yarn, 50 grams/131 yards (120m) per ball. I used Knit Picks Galileo, 50 percent merino, 50 percent viscose from bamboo.

Chart

Branching eyelet

Gauge (Tension)

Although gauge (tension) isn't crucial for this project, the suggested gauge (tension) is 22 stitches and 32 rows = 4 inches (10cm) in stockinette (stocking) stitch, after blocking.

Needles

U.S. 5 (3.75 mm/UK 9) straight needles

Other Supplies

2 stitch markers, blunt yarn needle

Construction Notes

If you want to make the scarf wider, increase your cast-on by multiples of 10.

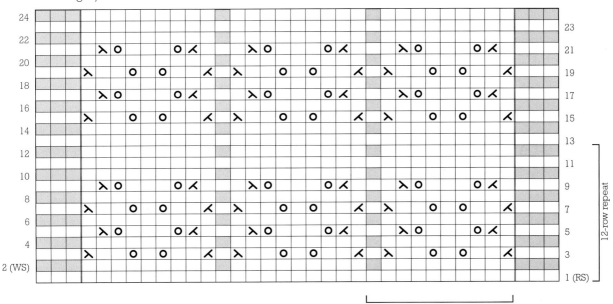

9-stitch panels separated by 1 stitch of garter
orange lines show position of markers

Legend/Key

☐ Knit on right side, purl on wrong side

▨ Purl on right side, knit on wrong side

◹ Knit 2 together on right side

◺ Slip-slip-knit 2 together on right side

◯ Yarn over on right side

Branching Eyelet Scarf

Cast on 35 stitches.

Work from the chart, repeating Rows 1 through 12 of the chart 40 times, ending on Row 11 instead of Row 12 on your last row. Or work from written instructions, as follows:

Row 1 (RS; marker set up): Knit 3, place a marker, knit until 3 sts remain on left needle, place a second marker, k3.

Row 2 and all WS rows: Knit 3 to marker, sm, p9, *k1, p9; rep from * to marker, sm, k3 to end.

Row 3: Knit to marker, sm, *k2tog, k2, yo, k1, yo, k2, ssk, k1; rep from * to marker, ending last rep with ssk, sm, k3.

Row 5: Knit to marker, sm, k1, *k2tog, yo, k3, yo, ssk, k3; rep from * to marker, ending last rep k1 instead of k3, sm, k3.

Row 7: Repeat Row 3.

Row 9: Repeat Row 5.

Row 11: Knit all stitches.

Row 12: Work 1 more WS row.

Repeat these 12 rows about 39 more times, or until the scarf is the desired length, stopping on Row 11 instead of Row 12 on the last repeat.

Bind (cast) off.

Finishing

Wet-block your scarf, and weave in the ends.

infinity lace
scarf

● ● ○ ○ ○

The scalloped edge naturally formed by the lace pattern adds a softness to this looped scarf that's worked in the round in a big ring. The lace pattern is a traditional favorite; it's simple to work but has beautiful results. You can wear this infinity scarf looped once or twice around your neck.

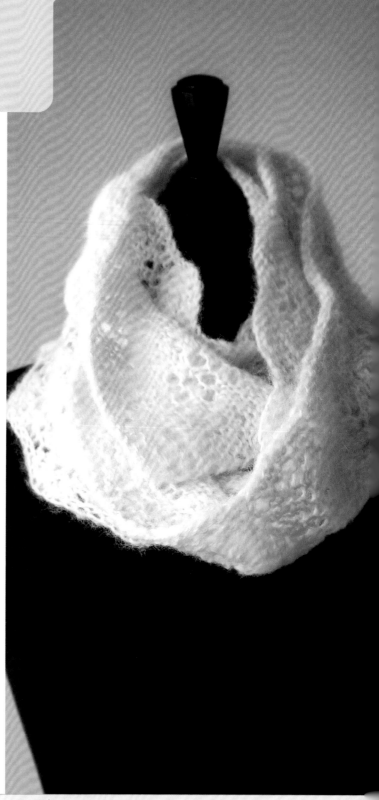

Skills Needed

Basic lace, working in the round

Finished Measurements

About 46 inches (117cm) around and 10 inches (25.5cm) high

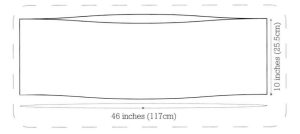

46 inches (117cm)

10 inches (25.5cm)

Chart

Traveling vine

Yarn

2 balls medium weight (worsted or aran) yarn, 50 grams/137 yards (125m) each. This pattern works best in a yarn with a soft, airy fiber blend, like baby alpaca, kid mohair, or angora. I used 80 percent baby alpaca, 20 percent acrylic.

Gauge (Tension)

16 stitches and 20 rows over 4 inches (10cm), in traveling vine pattern, blocked

Needles

U.S. 9 (5.5mm/UK 5) circular needles, about 24 inches (60cm) long

Other Supplies

Stitch marker, blunt yarn needle

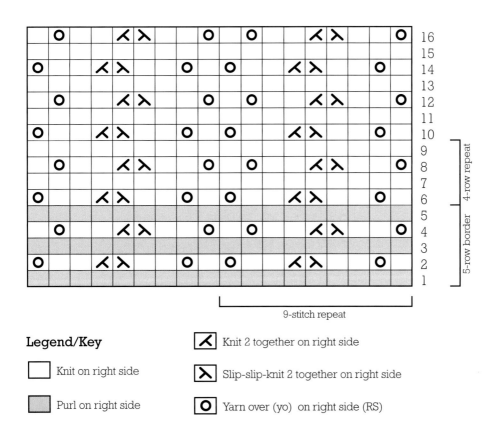

Legend/Key

☐ Knit on right side

▨ Purl on right side

⊼ Knit 2 together on right side

⊻ Slip-slip-knit 2 together on right side

◉ Yarn over (yo) on right side (RS)

Infinity Lace Scarf

Cast on 180 stitches. Being careful not to twist stitches, join for working in the round. Place a marker to show the beginning of the round.

Work 5 rounds as follows, or follow Rounds 1 through 5 of the chart:

Round 1: Purl all stitches.

Round 2: *Knit 1, yarn over, knit 2, slip-slip-knit, knit-2-together, knit 2, yarn over; repeat from * to end of round.

Round 3: You ended with a yarn over on Round 2, so your yarn is at the back. Bring the yarn to the front so the yarn over goes all the way around the needle. Purl all stitches.

Round 4: *Yarn over, knit 2, slip-slip-knit, knit-2-together, knit 2, yarn over, knit 1; repeat from * to end of round.

Round 5: Purl all stitches.

Now work 4 rounds as follows, or follow Rounds 6 through 9 of the chart:

Round 6: Repeat Round 2.

Round 7: Knit all stitches.

Round 8: Repeat Round 4.

Round 9: Knit all stitches.

Repeat Rounds 6 through 9 eight times.

Then repeat Rounds 6 through 8 once.

Then repeat Rounds 1 through 5.

Bind (cast) off loosely. Cut the yarn, leaving a long tail.

Finishing

Wet-block your scarf, and weave in your yarn tails.

- -

To modify the circumference of the scarf, change the cast-on in multiples of 9.

- -

buttoned
wristlets

● ● ○ ○ ○

These pretty fingerless mitts are a quick and easy project that use less than a single ball of yarn. Neat borders of seed (moss) stitch frame a lovely diamond brocade motif. This is a fun way to venture into mitts without knitting in the round or working individual thumbs and fingers, not to mention a great excuse to feature a couple cute buttons!

Skills Needed

Combining knits and purls, working mattress stitch, sewing on buttons

Finished Measurements

About 7 inches (18cm) around and 4½ inches (11.5cm) high

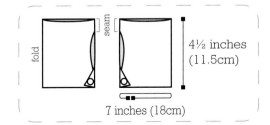

4½ inches (11.5cm)

fold

seam

7 inches (18cm)

Yarn

Half a ball of fine weight (sport or light DK) yarn, 50 grams/131 yards (120m). I used Knit Picks Galileo, 50 percent merino, 50 percent viscose from bamboo.

Chart

Gauge (Tension)

22 stitches and 32 rows = 4 inches (10cm) in brocade pattern

Needles

U.S. 5 (3.75 mm/UK 9) straight needles

Other Supplies

Blunt yarn needle, 2 stitch markers, 2 small buttons

Construction Notes

Each wristlet is worked as a flat rectangle, with a small yarn over buttonhole on the lower edge. Fold vertically and seam above the thumb. Try on to fit, and attach a button at the wrist. Left and right wristlets are almost identical; the only difference is the side where you work the buttonhole.

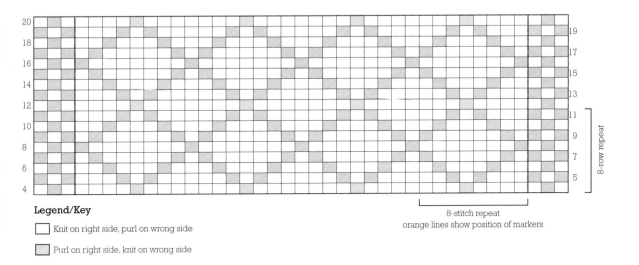

8-row repeat

Legend/Key

☐ Knit on right side, purl on wrong side

▨ Purl on right side, knit on wrong side

8-stitch repeat
orange lines show position of markers

Buttoned Wristlets

Cast on 39 stitches.

Work 3 rows of seed (moss) stitch with one buttonhole as follows:

Row 1 (RS): P1, *k1, p1; rep from * to end.

Right wristlet Row 2 (WS; buttonhole row):
P1, k1, yo, k2tog, p1, *k1, p1; rep from * to end.

Left wristlet Row 2 (WS; buttonhole row):
Work as Row 1 until 3 sts remain on left needle, yo, k2tog, p1.

Row 3: Work as Row 1 for 3 stitches, place marker, continue as Row 1 until 3 sts remain, place marker, and finish p1, k1, p1.

Work 33 rows of brocade with 3 stitches of seed (moss) stitch at each edge as follows, or work from the chart:

Row 4 (WS): P1, k1, p1 to marker, sm, p4, *k1, p7; rep from * to marker, ending last rep p4 instead of p7, sm, p1, k1, p1.

Row 5: P1, k1, p1 to marker, sm, k3, *p1, k1, p1, k5; rep from * to marker, ending last rep k3 instead of k5, sm, p1, k1, p1.

Row 6: P1, k1, p1, sm, p2, *k1, p3; rep from * to marker, ending last rep p2 instead of p3, sm, p1, k1, p1.

Row 7: P1, k1, p1, sm, k1, p1, *k5, p1, k1, p1; rep from * to marker, ending last rep [p1, k1] instead of [p1, k1, p1], sm, p1, k1, p1.

Row 8: P1, k1, p1, sm, k1, *p7, k1; rep from * to marker, sm, p1, k1, p1.

Row 9: Repeat Row 7.

Row 10: Repeat Row 6.

Row 11: Repeat Row 5.

Repeat Rows 4 through 11 three times.

Repeat Row 4 once.

Finish with 3 rows of seed (moss) stitch:

All 3 rows: P1, *k1, p1; rep from * to end.

Bind (cast) off, leaving a long tail for seaming.

Finishing

Block.

Fold in half vertically, with wrong sides facing, and join above the thumb hole: using mattress stitch and tail from bind off, sew from the top of the wristlet for ¾ inch (2cm). Try on wristlet to check how much overlap is needed at the wrist edge. Sew on a button at the wrist. Weave in any remaining ends.

textured gansey
scarf

●●●○○

Inspired by the traditional Guernsey fishermen's sweaters from the British Isles, this "gansey" scarf is a great project for the beginner knitter who is comfortable with knit-purl combinations. Simple geometric elements alternated with plain knitting create a striped effect. This scarf looks great in an earthy heather like the one shown here, but it's versatile enough for almost any color. Use a light or mid-toned color like this to show off the textures.

Skills Needed

Casting on, combining knits and purls

Finished Measurements

Approximately 7 inches (18cm) wide and 56 inches (142cm) long

Yarn

3 balls medium weight (worsted or aran) weight yarn, 50 grams/110 yards (100m) each. I used Knit Picks Swish Worsted, 100 percent superwash merino.

Gauge (Tension)

18 stitches and 24 rows = 4 inches (10cm) in stockinette (stocking) stitch, blocked. Gauge (tension) isn't crucial for this project.

Needles

U.S. 7 (4.5mm/UK 7) straight needles

Other Supplies

Blunt yarn needle, 2 stitch markers

Textured Gansey Scarf

There are quite a few rows in the pattern. But don't worry—the texture is simple and you'll be able to "read" your work easily after a few rows. If you want to keep track of where you are, keep a pencil handy and check off each row in the margin as you complete it, or use a sticky note to underline the row you're working on.

All the texture work is done from the wrong side. This means you have to pay attention when reading your stitches from the back, but the big advantage is that all right side rows are always knit, giving you a break every other row.

Cast on 32 stitches.

**

Rows 1 through 26: Work in garter zigzag as follows:

Row 1 (Right Side): Knit.

Row 2 (Wrong Side): On this row, you establish the 3-stitch garter stitch edges and begin the zigzag texture. Knit 3, place a marker. Purl 1, *knit 3, purl 3; repeat from * until 4 stitches remain, purl 1. Place a second marker, knit 3.

Row 3 and all Right Side rows: Knit, slipping markers as you encounter them.

Row 4: Knit to marker, slip marker to the right needle, purl 2, *knit 3, purl 3; repeat from * to the second marker, slip marker, knit 3.

Row 6: Knit to marker, slip marker, purl 3, *knit 3, purl 3; repeat from * to the second marker, ending last repeat purl 2 instead of purl 3, slip marker, knit 3.

Row 8: Knit to marker, slip marker, purl 4, *knit 3, purl 3; repeat from * to the second marker, ending last repeat purl 1 instead of purl 3, slip marker, knit 3.

Row 10: Repeat Row 6.

Row 12: Repeat Row 4.

Rows 13 through 24: Repeat Rows 1 through 12 once.

Rows 25 and 26: Repeat Rows 1 and 2 once.

Rows 27 through 30: Knit 4 rows, slipping the markers as you encounter them. (This makes 2 ridges of garter stitch.)

Rows 31 through 38: Work in stockinette (stocking) stitch, as follows:

Right Side rows: Knit.

Wrong Side rows: Knit to marker, slip marker, purl to second marker, slip marker, knit to end.

Rows 39 through 42: Knit 4 rows.

Rows 43 through 52: Work in double-dot stitch, as follows:

Row 43 and all Right Side rows: Knit.

Row 44: Knit to marker, slip marker, purl 1, *knit 2, purl 2; repeat from * until 4 stitches remain, purl 1, slip marker, knit 3.

Row 46: Knit to marker, slip marker, purl 3, *knit 2, purl 2; repeat from * to marker, ending last repeat purl 1 instead of purl 2, slip marker, knit 3.

Rows 47 through 50: Repeat Rows 43 through 46 once.

Rows 51 and 52: Repeat Rows 43 and 44 once.

Rows 53 through 56: Knit 4 rows.

Rows 57 through 64: Repeat Rows 31 through 38 to make another dividing band of stockinette (stocking) stitch.

Rows 65 through 68: Knit 4 rows.

Now go back to the ** and repeat Rows 1 through 68 four more times. Or five more times if you like a very long scarf.

You're almost done! Finish by repeating Rows 1 through 26.

Bind (cast) off.

Finishing

Block your scarf, and weave in your yarn ends.

If you want to make the scarf wider, increase the cast-on in multiples of 12. Note that a wider scarf will require more yarn.

eyelet triangular
shawl

● ● ● ○ ○

I used to think of shawls as old-fashioned accessories, suitable for genteel Victorian ladies, but the shawl has evolved and become a versatile item with incredible variety. You can use lace or tweed yarn, chunky or fine, as traditional or as modern as you like. This top-down triangular shawl is simple, elegant, and versatile. Once you get the hang of the construction, you might want to explore more elaborate designs in finer yarn.

Skills Needed

Combining knits and purls, increasing, wet-blocking

Finished Measurements

About 58 inches (147cm) wide and 29 inches (74cm) high

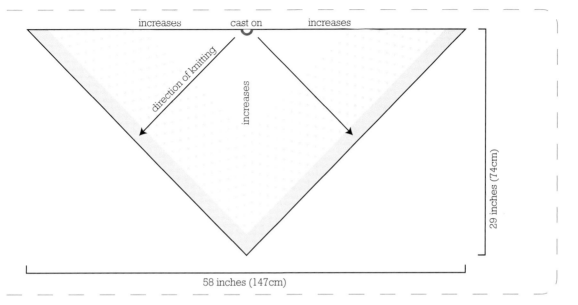

Yarn

5 balls fine (sport or light DK) yarn, 50 grams/110 yards (100m) per ball. I used Knit Picks Andean Treasure, 100 percent baby alpaca.

Gauge (Tension)

20 stitches and 30 rows = 4 inches (10cm) in stockinette (stocking) stitch, blocked. Gauge (tension) isn't crucial for this project, but a different gauge (tension) will affect the final dimensions of your shawl.

Needles

U.S. 7 (4.5mm/UK 7) circular needles

This is larger than you would usually use with fine yarn, but the goal is to have relatively open stitches.

Other Supplies

Stitch marker, blunt yarn needle

Construction Notes

The first time you make a top-down triangular shawl like this, some of the construction might seem counterintuitive, and you may have moments of doubt: how will this strange shape turn into a tidy triangle? Don't worry. Geometry and blocking bring it all together. You work the shawl flat, back and forth, on circular needles to accommodate the long rows, from the middle of the top edge and out to the tips. The rows begin very short and increase at an even rate. The final isosceles shape is achieved by wet-blocking your shawl. The wet-block is relatively aggressive, and you stretch your knitting much more than you would for say, a sweater.

Eyelet Triangular Shawl

Using a knitted or half-hitch method and leaving a long tail, cast on 10 stitches.

Set up row (Wrong Side): K2, p3, place marker for center, p3, k2.

Row 1 (Right Side; Inc): K2, kfb twice, k1, slip marker, kfb twice, k3—4 increased, 14 stitches.

Row 2 (WS): K2, purl to last 2 sts, slipping center marker, k2.

Row 3 (Inc): K2, kfb, knit to 2 sts before marker, kfb, k1, slip marker, kfb, knit to 4 sts before end, kfb, k3—4 increased, 18 stitches.

Row 4: Repeat Row 2.

Work 44 more rows as set by Rows 3 and 4—106 stitches.

Begin eyelet section:

Row 1 of eyelet section (RS): K2, kfb, k3, yo, k2tog, *k4, yo, k2tog; rep from * stopping 3 sts before marker, k1, kfb, k1, slip marker, kfb, k3, yo, k2tog, *k4, yo, k2tog; rep from *, stopping 5 sts before end, k1, kfb, k3—4 increased, 110 stitches.

Rows 2 through 6 of eyelet section: Work as set by Rows 3 and 4—8 increased, 118 stitches.

Repeat the last 6 rows 9 more times—108 increased, 226 stitches.

And end with a garter stitch border:

Next row (WS; garter ridge): K2, p1, knit to 1 before marker, p1, slip marker, p1, knit to 3 before end, p1, k2.

Work 19 more rows, working all WS as garter ridges and all RS as set by Row 3—40 increased, 266 stitches.

Bind (cast) off on the wrong side; as you bind (cast) off, keep your tension quite loose. The goal is for the edge to have enough slack to stretch with the garter stitch border when you block. To be sure the edge is loose enough as you go, give your bound (cast) off edge a little pull. If it's too tight, the garter stitch border will buckle.

Finishing

Whip stitch the cast-on edge closed. Wet-block the shawl, pinning it into triangular shape. Weave in ends.

Before you block, your shawl might look more like a diamond.

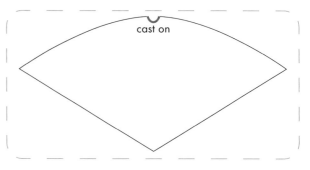

cast on

fair isle fingerless
mitts

● ● ● ● ●

This project introduces you to stranded colorwork in the round. If you've admired traditional Fair Isle knitting but are unsure about how difficult it is, this small-scale project will help demystify the process for you. These mitts combine working in the round, ribbing, plain knitting, and stranded knitting. A simplified thumb with a raw bound (cast) off edge keeps the fussiness to a minimum. The three-color motif around the cuff uses the Fair Isle tradition of introducing a color shift at the halfway point, but you could simplify this by using only two colors.

Skills Needed

Combining knits and purls, using m1L and m1R (make 1 left and right), working in the round, working from a chart, stranding colors

Finished Measurements

To fit Adult Small (Medium, Large), about 6½ (7¼, 8¼) inches (16.5 [18.75, 21] cm) around and 7 inches (18cm) high

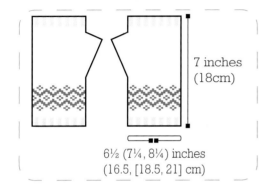

7 inches (18cm)

6½ (7¼, 8¼) inches (16.5, [18.5, 21] cm)

Yarn

3 balls (1 each of Main Color [MC] and contrasting Colors A and B) fine weight (sport or light DK) yarn, 50 grams/131 yards (120 m). I used Knit Picks Galileo, 50 percent merino, 50 percent viscose from bamboo.

Gauge (Tension)

26 stitches and 31 rows = 4 inches (10cm) in stockinette (stocking) stitch, blocked

Needles

1 set in your preferred method for working in a small round: U.S. 4 (3.5mm/UK 9 or 10) or size needed to obtain gauge or U.S. 3 (3.25mm/UK 10 or 11)

Other Supplies

Blunt yarn needle, 3 stitch markers, cable needle

Construction Notes

Each mitt is worked in the round from the cuff up. Working with two colors at once can affect your gauge (tension), especially when you're working in the round. To keep this project manageable, I've only included a few rounds of colorwork, so you have to pay special attention to your gauge (tension) when transitioning from the colorwork to plain knitting. Before starting, it's worth trying out a few repeats of the chart in the round, followed by a few rounds of stockinette (stocking) stitch. If you find your colorwork is pulling in, you can use larger needles for that part. Wet-blocking gives you a chance to shape the mitts a little more.

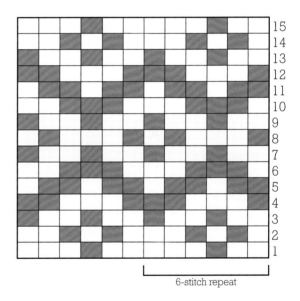

6-stitch repeat

Legend/Key

Knit all stitches

☐ Main Color (MC)

▨ Color A

☐ Color B

Chart

Fair Isle Fingerless Mitts

Work 2 the same.

With MC and smaller needles, cast on 40 (48, 52) stitches. Arrange for working in the round and join, being careful not to twist your stitches. Place a marker for the beginning of the round.

Work 6 rounds of 2/2 ribbing:

All rounds: *K2, p2; rep from * to end.

Switch to larger needles.

Small (Large) only:

Next round (increase stitch count to fit chart multiple of 6): M1R, k20 (26), m1R, knit to end—2 increased, 42 (54) stitches.

Knit 1 round.

Medium only:

Knit 2 rounds.

All sizes:

Work 15 rounds from the chart.

Continue in MC from here.

Work thumb:

Next round (Inc; thumb marker setup): K1, m1R, place marker for one side of thumb, knit to 1 stitch before end of round, place marker for opposite side of thumb, m1L, k1— 2 increased, 44 (50, 56) stitches.

*Knit 2 rounds, slipping markers as you come to them.

Next round (Inc): Knit to first thumb marker, m1R, sm, knit to second thumb marker, sm, m1L, knit to end of round—2 increased, 46 (52, 58) stitches.

Repeat from * 3 (4, 5) more times—6 (8, 10) increased, 52 (60, 68) stitches.

Knit 1 round.

Next round (Dec; bind off thumb): Knit to second thumb marker, remove it, knit 1 (you should have 5 [6, 7] stitches remaining before the end of round). Bind off the next 10 (12, 14) stitches, removing beg of rnd marker—42 (48, 54) stitches.

Next round: Knit to 1 stitch before end.

Next round (join): This round starts off with a little knitting acrobatics to minimize loose stitches at the join. Slip the last, unworked stitch of the previous round onto your cable needle and hold in back. Knit 1, replace marker for beg of round, and knit 1 from cable needle. Knit to end.

Small (Large) only:

Next round (decrease stitch count to fit 2/2 rib multiple of 4): K2tog, k19 (25), k2tog, knit to end—2 decreased, 40 (52) stitches.

Medium only:

Knit 1 round.

Switch to smaller needles, and work 6 rounds of 2/2 ribbing:

All rounds: *K2, p2; rep from * to end.

Bind (cast) off. When binding (casting) off, try to match the tension of the ribbing so the top of the mitts don't flare out.

Finishing

Wet-block mitts, and weave in ends.

- -

Try playing with your own color themes; you could switch around the contrast by making the background dark and the motif light. Or try a neutral set in grays and creamy undyed wool. These mitts work for men or women.

- -

cabled
headband

A headband is a fun way to try out your new cabling skills! A small project like this is quick to finish and versatile, too. You can wear it as a hair band to dress up a hairstyle or as an ear warmer in winter.

Skills Needed

Combining knits and purls, making basic cables, joining with whip stitch

Finished Measurements

About 19 inches (48cm) around, unstretched, and 4 inches (10cm) at widest point

Yarn

1 ball medium weight (worsted or aran) weight yarn, 50 grams/110 yards (100m) each. I used Knit Picks Swish Worsted, 100 percent superwash merino.

Gauge (Tension)

24 stitches and 24 rows = 4 inches (10cm) in cable and rib pattern, blocked

Needles

U.S. 7 (4.5mm/UK 7) straight needles

Other Supplies

Cable needle, blunt yarn needle

Construction Notes

The headband is worked flat and joined at the center back. The band is slightly shaped to be wider at the top of the head.

Special Stitches Used

Back-cross-4-cable: Hold the next 2 stitches in the back on the cable needle, knit 2, and knit 2 from the cable needle.

Front-cross-4-cable: Hold the next 2 stitches in the front on the cable needle, knit 2, and knit 2 from the cable needle.

Cabled Headband

Cast on 18 stitches.

Row 1 (RS): K2, *p2, k2; repeat from *.

Row 2: P2, *k2, p2; repeat from *.

Repeat Rows 1 and 2 three more times.

Next row (RS; Inc): [K2, p2] twice, m1R, k2, m1L, [p2, k2] twice—20 sts.

Next row: [P2, k2] twice, p4, [k2, p2] twice.

Next row: [K2, p2] twice, k4, [p2, k2] twice.

Continue as established by the last 2 rows for 5 more rows.

Next row (RS; Inc): [K2, p2] twice, k1, m1R, k2, m1L, k1, [p2, k2] twice—22 sts.

Next row: [P2, k2] twice, p6, [k2, p2] twice.

Next row: [K2, p2] twice, k6, [p2, k2] twice.

Continue as established by the last 2 rows for 5 more rows.

Next row (RS; Inc): [K2, p2] twice, k2, m1R, k2, m1L, k2, [p2, k2] twice—24 sts.

Next row: [P2, k2] twice, p8, [k2, p2] twice.

**

Next row (RS; cable row): [K2, p2] twice, back-cross-4-cable, front-cross-4-cable, [p2, k2] twice.

Next row: [P2, k2] twice, p8, [k2, p2] twice.

Next row: [K2, p2] twice, k8, [p2, k2] twice.

Continue as established by the last 2 rows for 3 more rows.

Repeat from ** five more times.

**

Next row (RS; reverse the direction of the cables): [K2, p2] twice, front-cross-4-cable, back-cross-4-cable, [p2, k2] twice.

Work 5 rows without cabling as established.

Repeat from ** five more times.

Next row (RS; Dec): [K2, p2] twice, ssk, k4, k2tog, [p2, k2] twice—22 sts.

Next row: [P2, k2] twice, p6, [k2, p2] twice.

Next row: [K2, p2] twice, k6, [p2, k2] twice.

Continue as established by the last 2 rows for 5 more rows.

Next row (RS; Dec): [K2, p2] twice, ssk, k2, k2tog, [p2, k2] twice—20 sts.

Next row: [P2, k2] twice, p4, [k2, p2] twice.

Next row: [K2, p2] twice, k4, [p2, k2] twice.

Continue as established by the last 2 rows for 5 more rows.

Next row (RS; Dec): [K2, p2] twice, ssk, k2tog, [p2, k2] twice—18 sts.

Next row: P2, *k2, p2; repeat from *.

Next row: K2, *p2, k2; repeat from *.

Continue as established by the last 2 rows for 5 more rows.

Do a measurement check: wrap the band around your (or the intended wearer's) head. Slightly stretched, the two ends should meet. If necessary, work more rows in K2/P2 ribbing to get the desired fit.

Bind (cast) off.

Finishing

Block and then whip stitch the ends together from both the right and wrong sides. The finished seam will be visible, but it'll be strong and flat. Weave in the ends.

cabled
hat

● ● ● ○ ○

Allover braided cables on stockinette (stocking) stitch make a scrumptious fabric. This is a versatile hat, and you can easily customize it to suit men, women, or youth. For a younger wearer, try making the hat slouchier by working an extra repeat of the cable pattern. For a traditional toque, you can work twice as many rows of ribbing for a folded rim. And for a whimsical wintery look, try topping it with a pom-pom or tassel.

Skills Needed

Working in the round, simple cables

Finished Measurements

To fit Youth or Adult Small (Medium, Large), about 18¾ (20¼, 22) inches (47.5 [51.5, 56] cm) around, slightly stretched, and 6½ inches (16.5cm) from brim to crown.

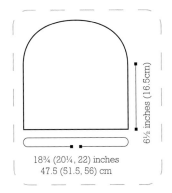

18¾ (20¼, 22) inches
47.5 (51.5, 56) cm

6½ inches (16.5cm)

Chart

Braided cable chart

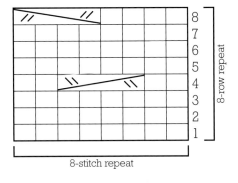

8-row repeat

8-stitch repeat

Yarn

1 skein medium weight (worsted or aran) yarn, 100 grams/220 yards (201m). I used Knit Picks Swish Worsted, 100 percent superwash merino wool.

Gauge (Tension)

20.5 stitches and 28 rows = 4 inches (10cm) in cable pattern, blocked

Needles

1 set each, in your preferred method for working in a small round: U.S. 6 (4mm/UK 8) and U.S. 7 (4.5mm/UK 7), or size needed to obtain gauge

Other Supplies

Cable needle, blunt yarn needle, stitch marker

Construction Notes

The hat is worked from the bottom up in the round.

Legend/Key

☐ Knit

⟋⟋ Cable 4 back: slip next 2 sts to cable needle, hold in back, knit 2, knit 2 from cable needle

⟍⟍ Cable 4 front: slip next 2 sts to cable needle, hold in front, knit 2, knit 2 from cable needle

Cabled Hat

With smaller needles, cast on 96 (104, 112) stitches. Arrange stitches for working in the round, being careful not to twist, and place a marker for the beginning of the round.

Work 10 Rounds of 2/2 ribbing:

All rounds of 2/2 ribbing: *K2, p2; repeat from * to end of round.

Switch to larger needles.

Work 40 rounds as follows, or work 5 repeats from the chart:

Rounds 1 through 3 of braided cable: Knit all stitches.

Round 4: K2, *cable 4 back (slip next 2 sts to cable needle, hold in back, knit 2, knit 2 from cable needle), k4; rep from *, ending last repeat k2 instead of k4.

Rounds 5 through 7: Knit all stitches.

Round 8: *K4, cable 4 front (slip next 2 sts to cable needle, hold in front, knit 2, knit 2 from cable needle); rep from * to end of round.

Repeat Rounds 1 through 8 four more times.

Work the crown:

Round 1 of crown (Dec): K5, *k2tog, k6; rep from *, ending last repeat k1 instead of k6—12 (13, 14) decreased, 84 (91, 98) sts.

Round 2: Knit all stitches.

Round 3 (Dec): K4, *k2tog, k5; rep from *, ending last repeat k1 instead of k5—12 (13, 14) decreased, 72 (78, 84) sts.

Round 4: Knit all stitches.

Round 5 (Dec): K3, *k2tog, k4; rep from *, ending last repeat k1 instead of k4—12 (13, 14) decreased, 60 (65, 70) sts.

Round 6 (Dec): K2, *k2tog, k3; rep from *, ending last repeat k1 instead of k3—12 (13, 14) decreased, 48 (52, 56) sts.

Round 7 (Dec): K1, *k2tog, k2; rep from *, ending last repeat k1 instead of k2—12 (13, 14) decreased, 36 (39, 42) sts.

Round 8 (Dec): *K2tog, k1; rep from * to end—12 (13, 14) decreased, 24 (26, 28) sts.

Cut the yarn and using your blunt yarn needle, thread the tail through the remaining stitches and slip them off the knitting needles. Draw the tail tight and thread it to the wrong side.

Finishing

Block the hat, and weave in yarn ends.

If you like, top off your hat with a matching tassel.

friendly
critters

● ● ● ● ○

Adorable, squishy, and petite, each one of these fun critters starts with the same basic recipe. You add the personality with strategic color changes and a few finishing details. Simply change an ear, nose, or tail, and you have a different animal. The body is slightly wedge-shaped, so the critter sits upright.

Skills Needed

Basic sewing, working with stripes, picking up stitches, I-cord

Finished Measurements

About 5 inches (13cm) wide at the base and 5 inches (13cm) high

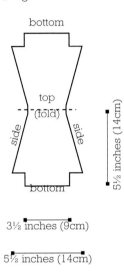

bottom

top
(fold)

side   side

5½ inches (14cm)

bottom

3½ inches (9cm)

5½ inches (14cm)

Yarn

Each critter requires about 35 grams/39 yards (35m) bulky (chunky, 12-ply) weight yarn. I used a mix of yarns. Wool blends work best for this project. You can use multiple strands of finer yarns held together to get a bulky (chunky, 12-ply) weight.

Colors needed:

Cat: Natural, Yellow

Raccoon: Gray, Black, Natural

Panda: Natural, Black

Gauge (Tension)

12 stitches and 17 rows = 4 inches (10cm) in stockinette (stocking) stitch. Gauge (tension) isn't crucial for this project, but aim for a tight gauge (tension) so the stuffing doesn't show through.

Needles

U.S. 8 (5mm/UK 6) straights and dpns

Other Supplies

Blunt yarn needle

Stuffing

For the faces: crafting felt, white craft glue, wooden toothpicks, sharp needle, and embroidery floss

Construction Notes

Each critter's body is worked flat, joined at the sides, stuffed, and then joined at the bottom edge and corners. The color scheme for each critter is noted in the pattern. The arms and legs are knitted I-cord tubes. The ears are knitted, and the facial features are added with a combination of felt and simple contrast hand-stitching.

Although these critters are soft and friendly, they do have small parts, so they're not suitable for very young children and babies.

Friendly Critter

Body

Use the color guide as you knit each body. You can also use the color guide as a checklist as you complete each row.

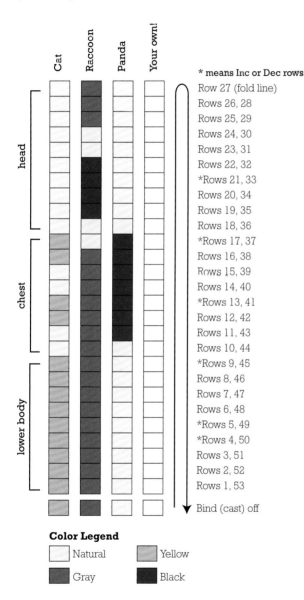

* means Inc or Dec rows

Row 27 (fold line)
Rows 26, 28
Rows 25, 29
Rows 24, 30
Rows 23, 31
Rows 22, 32
*Rows 21, 33
Rows 20, 34
Rows 19, 35
Rows 18, 36
*Rows 17, 37
Rows 16, 38
Rows 15, 39
Rows 14, 40
*Rows 13, 41
Rows 12, 42
Rows 11, 43
Rows 10, 44
*Rows 9, 45
Rows 8, 46
Rows 7, 47
Rows 6, 48
*Rows 5, 49
*Rows 4, 50
Rows 3, 51
Rows 2, 52
Rows 1, 53
Bind (cast) off

Color Legend

- Natural
- Gray
- Yellow
- Black

Cast on 13 stitches.

Row 1 (RS): Knit to end.

Row 2 (WS): Purl.

Row 3: Knit.

Row 4 (Inc): Purl to end, cast on 4 using half-hitch—17 sts.

Row 5 (Inc): Knit to end, cast on 4 using half-hitch—21 sts.

Rows 6, 7, 8: Purl WS and knit RS rows.

Row 9 (Dec): K1, k2tog, knit to last 3 sts, ssk, k1—19 sts.

Rows 10, 11, 12: Purl WS and knit RS rows.

Row 13 (Dec): Repeat Row 9—17 sts.

Rows 14, 15, 16: Purl WS and knit RS rows.

Row 17 (Dec): Repeat Row 9—15 sts.

Rows 18, 19, 20: Purl WS and knit RS rows.

Row 21 (Dec): Repeat Row 9—13 sts.

Rows 22 through 32: Purl WS and knit RS rows. Row 27 is the fold line for the top of the head.

Row 33 (Inc): K1, m1R, knit to last st, m1L, k1—15 sts.

Rows 34, 35, 36: Purl WS and knit RS rows.

Row 37 (Inc): Repeat Row 33—17 sts.

Rows 38, 39, 40: Purl WS and knit RS rows.

Row 41 (Inc): Repeat Row 33—19 sts.

Rows 42, 43, 44: Purl WS and knit RS rows.

Row 45 (Inc): Repeat Row 33—21 sts.

Rows 46, 47, 48: Purl WS and knit RS rows.

Row 49: Bind (cast) off 4, knit to end—17 sts.

Row 50: Bind (cast) off 4, purl to end—13 sts.

Rows 51, 52, 53: Purl WS and knit RS rows.

Bind (cast) off.

Finishing

Weave in all yarn ends, except for one long tail from the bound (cast) off edge. You only need to weave in enough to secure the ends; everything will be hidden.

Fold the body in half at the fold line, with WS facing. Join the sides with mattress stitch. When dealing with stripes, use the lightest color to join, and take care to line up the stripes.

Stuff the body and then join the bottom seam with mattress stitch, using one of the yarn tails. Join the corners using mattress stitch.

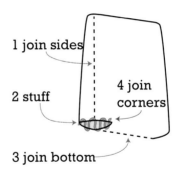

For each critter's details, use the photo as a guide. Be as creative as you like: change the size of ears, length of limbs, or facial details to personalize your critter.

Arms

Work both arms the same: With dpn and (Cat: Natural, Raccoon: Gray, Panda: Black) yarn, 1½ inches (3.75cm) from top, pick up and knit 4 stitches across side seam. Knit 7 rows of I-cord. Bind (cast) off.

Legs

Work both legs the same: With dpn and (Cat: Yellow, Raccoon: Gray, Panda: Black) yarn, pick up and knit 4 stitches across the bottom front corner. Knit 8 rows of I-cord. Cat only: With Natural, knit 2 rows. All critters: Bind (cast) off.

Ears

Cat (using Natural):

Right ear: From back, starting at top-right corner, pick up and knit 5 stitches across top of head.

Rows 1 and 3 (RS): Purl.

Row 2: K3, k2tog—4 sts.

Row 4: Ssk, k2tog—2 sts.

Row 5: K2tog.

Thread the tail through the last stitch.

Left ear: From back, starting 5 stitches in from top-left corner (mirroring right ear), pick up and knit 5.

Rows 1 and 3 (RS): Purl.

Row 2: Ssk, k3—4 sts.

Row 4: Ssk, k2tog—2 sts.

Row 5: Ssk—1 st.

Thread the tail through the last stitch.

Raccoon (using Gray):

Right ear: From back, pick up and knit 5 stitches around top-right corner. Work the same as Cat right ear.

Left ear: From back, pick up and knit 5 stitches around top left-corner (mirroring left ear). Work the same as Cat left ear.

Panda (using Black):

Work 2 the same: Cast on 3.

Row 1 (Inc): Kfb 3 times—6 sts.

Row 2: Knit.

Row 3: K1, kfb, k2, kfb, k1—8 sts.

Bind (cast) off, leaving a long tail.

With tail, whip stitch each ear along top corner of head.

Tail

With dpn and (Cat: Yellow, Raccoon: Gray, Panda: Natural) yarn, pick up and knit 3 stitches across center-bottom edge. Work I-cord as follows:

Cat: Knit 7 rows.

Panda: Knit 2 rows.

Raccoon: Knit 1 row Gray. Next row: With Natural, kfb, k1, kfb. Knit 1 row Natural, 2 rows Gray, 2 rows Natural, 2 rows Gray. Next row: With Gray, k2tog, k1, k2tog. Knit 1 row. Next row: K2tog, k1. Next row: K2tog.

Bind (cast) off.

Face

Have fun with the faces, using the photos as a guide, or make your own designs!

If you can, test-glue some felt pieces to fabric or scrap felt to get an idea of how much glue you need to use. Cut out the facial features and lay them out on the critter before gluing. Use toothpicks to spread a thin layer of glue on back of felt and carefully transfer to critter. Press gently on felt with the blunt end of a toothpick or your finger. Let dry.

When embroidering, use simple straight stitches and insert your needle between, not through, yarn strands.

striped
baby hat

Babies can pull off the most whimsical accessories, giving you the perfect opportunity to knit something fun like this easy hat with sporty stripes and jaunty tassels. It finishes so quickly, you'll want to make more than one! The stripes use small amounts of yarn, so this is a great project for using up your leftover yarn.

Skills Needed

Working in stripes, mattress stitch to join seams

Finished Measurements

Baby 0 to 6 months: circumference 15 inches (38cm), height 6½ inches (16.5cm)

Yarn

Medium (worsted, aran) weight yarn, 1 full ball, 50 grams/110 yards (101m), in Main Color, plus partial balls in 2 contrasting colors: 30 yards (27.5m) Color A, and 10 yards (9m) Color B. I used Knit Picks Swish Worsted, 100 percent superwash merino.

Gauge (Tension)

18 stitches and 26 rows = 4 inches (10cm) in stockinette (stocking) stitch after blocking

Needles

U.S. 7 (4.5mm/UK 7) straight or circular needles

Other Supplies

Blunt yarn needle, cardboard 2½ inches (6.25cm) square for making tassels

Construction Notes

You knit the hat sideways in a rectangle and then fold it across the crown and seam it at the sides. You can add the optional tassels at the top corners after you sew the side seams.

Hat—before finishing

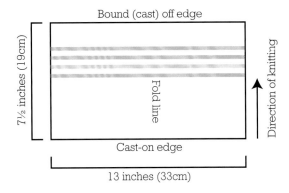

Hat—after finishing

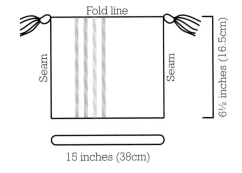

Striped Baby Hat

With Main Color, cast on 60 stitches. Leave a long tail; you'll use it to sew the side later.

Row 1 (Right Side): Knit across.

Row 2 (Wrong Side): Knit 5, purl until 5 stitches remain on left needle, knit 5.

Work 22 more rows following the pattern set up in Rows 1 and 2.

Then continue as established, but begin 14 rows of stripes as follows:

Join Color A, work 2 rows. Cut Color A.

With Main Color, work 2 rows. When working stripes, remember to carry the color you're working to the right and over the previous color.

Join Color B, work 2 rows. Cut Color B.

With Main Color, work 2 rows.

Join Color A, work 2 rows.

With Main Color, work 2 rows.

With Color A, work 2 rows. Cut Color A.

Finish with 10 rows in Main Color.

Bind (cast) off. Cut the yarn, leaving a long tail.

Finishing

Block hat and weave in ends (except the two long tails). Fold hat in half, wrong sides facing each other, and sew the sides using the long tails and mattress stitch. Join a tassel to each corner.

Want to modify the size? For every 1 inch (2.5cm) you want to add to the circumference, work 6 or 7 extra rows. For every 1 inch (2.5cm) you want to add to the height, cast on 9 extra stitches.

Quick and easy tassels

To make a tassel, wrap the yarn around the cardboard about 20 times, and cut the yarn. With your yarn needle, thread a piece of yarn under all the wraps, and tie it tight at the top.

Carefully slide everything off the cardboard. Wrap a piece of yarn about $^3/_4$ inch (2cm) from the top five times, and tie it tight.

Trim the bottom of the tassel to open the loops, and tidy any ragged ends.

striped baby
jacket

Knitting for babies is a delight. Babies are small, cute, and undiscerning and look great in anything. This sweater is a great way to practice for knitting an adult-size sweater. It also matches the Striped Baby Hat earlier in the book. The contrasting stripes make this extra cute, but feel free to use only one color.

Skills Needed

Working in stripes, increasing and decreasing, sewing on buttons

Finished Measurements

Chest (buttoned): 19 (20, 21) inches (48.25 [50.75, 53.25] cm), to fit 6 (12, 18) months

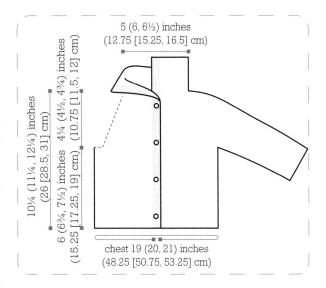

5 (6, 6½) inches (12.75 [15.25, 16.5] cm)

10¼ (11¼, 12¼) inches (26 [28.5, 31] cm)

4¼ (4½, 4¾) inches (10.75 [11.5, 12] cm)

6 (6¾, 7½) inches (15.25 [17.25, 19] cm)

chest 19 (20, 21) inches (48.25 [50.75, 53.25] cm)

Yarn

3 (4, 5) balls worsted weight yarn, 50 grams/110 yards (100.5m) each: 2 (3, 3) balls in Main Color, 1 (1, 2) in Color A. I used Knit Picks Swish Worsted, 100 percent superwash merino.

Gauge (Tension)

18 stitches and 26 rows = 4 inches (10cm) in stockinette (stocking) stitch, after blocking

Needles

Circular needles, about 24 inches long, plus needles for knitting in a small round using your favorite method in the following size: U.S. 7 (4.5mm/7 UK) or size needed to obtain gauge (tension)

Other Supplies

6 stitch markers, blunt yarn needle, smooth scrap yarn for holding stitches, 4 small buttons

Construction Notes

This is one of the simplest sweater constructions, with a seamless, top-down, raglan yoke. It's easy to knit and comfortable. Seamless means you knit all parts of the sweater together; the only thing you have to sew are the buttons. Top-down means you start at the neck and work down. Raglan means the sleeves fit into the body at an angle. The yoke is the part of the sweater that goes around the upper chest and arms, from just above the underarm all the way to the neckline.

Striped Baby Jacket

Collar

With Main Color, cast on 51 (59, 63) sts.

Knit 6 rows.

Next row (RS; marker set up for front bands): Knit 5, place marker, knit until 5 stitches remain on left needle, place marker, knit 5.

Next row (WS): Knit to marker, sm, purl to final marker, sm, knit to end.

Next row: Knit all stitches, slipping markers as you encounter them.

For 11 more rows, continue as established by these 2 rows.

Yoke

The first row after the collar begins the yoke and is where you place 4 more markers for the raglan increases.

First row (RS): Knit to marker, sm, k6 (7, 7) (left front), pm, k6 (8, 10) (left sleeve), pm, k17 (19, 19) (back), pm, k6 (8, 10) (right sleeve), pm, k6 (7, 7) (right front), sm, knit to end.

Next row (WS): Knit to first marker, sm, purl to final marker (slipping markers as you come to them), sm, knit to end.

Next row (RS; Inc): Knit to first marker, sm, *knit to 2 sts before next marker, kfb, k1, sm, kfb; rep from * 3 more times, then knit to end, slipping final marker—8 increased, 59 (67, 71) sts.

For 7 more rows, continue as established, increasing 8 sts every RS —24 increased, 83 (91, 95) sts.

Next row (RS; first buttonhole): Knit to first marker, sm, work to final marker, increasing 8 sts as usual, slip final marker, k1, k2tog, yo, k2—8 increased, 91 (99, 103) sts.

For 13 more rows, continue as established, increasing 8 sts every RS—139 (147, 151) sts.

Next row (RS; second buttonhole): Work as for first buttonhole—147 (155, 159) sts.

Work 1 more WS row.

Separate Sleeves from Body

Now comes the fun part, where your knitting starts to look like a sweater. You're going to put the sleeve stitches aside and join the back to the fronts and work the body to the bottom of the sweater.

Next row (RS): Cut two 18-inch (46cm) pieces of scrap yarn. Thread one on to your blunt needle, and set aside. Knit to the second marker, and remove marker. With your blunt needle, transfer the sleeve stitches to the scrap yarn and remove third marker.

Tie the ends of the scrap yarn together. Using the half-hitch cast-on, add 4 (6, 8) sts to the right needle. These are the underarm stitches. Knit across the back to the next marker, and remove it.

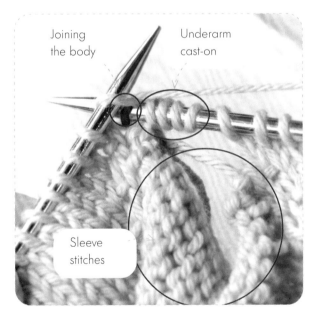

Joining the body

Underarm cast-on

Sleeve stitches

Transfer the next sleeve to the second piece of scrap yarn, tie the ends, remove the next marker. Cast on 4 (6, 8) sts for the next underarm. Knit to the end.

You now have 95 (103, 107) sts on the needles and 2 markers.

Here is how your sweater looks after completing the yoke and separating the sleeves.

Next row (WS): Knit to marker, sm, purl to last marker, sm, knit to end.

Continue as established for 10 more rows.

On the next RS row, work a third buttonhole.

Work 3 rows in Main Color.

Begin stripes:

Join A and work 2 rows in A, 2 rows Main Color, 2 rows A, 2 rows Main Color. The rest of the sweater is finished in A.

Work 2 rows.

On the next RS row, work the fourth and final buttonhole.

Do a measurement check: lay your work flat and carefully measure the length of the body from the underarm. Then continue, ending on a right side row, until the body measures 5 (5¾, 6½) inches (12.5 [14.5, 16.5] cm) from the underarms.

Knit 6 rows.

Bind (cast) off, removing markers.

Sleeves

Work both sleeves the same.

Transfer the sleeve stitches from your scrap yarn to your needles for knitting in a small round.

With Main Color, carefully pick up and knit 2 (3, 4) from the body's underarm edge (half underarm), place a marker, pick up and knit 2 (3, 4).

Then knit to the marker—34 (38, 42) sts.

Knit 13 rounds.

Next round (Dec): Knit 2, k2tog, knit to 4 sts before marker, ssk, k2—2 decreased, 32 (36, 40) sts.

Knit 1 round.

Begin stripes:

Join A and work 2 rounds in A, 2 rounds Main Color, 2 rounds A, 2 rounds Main Color. The rest of the sleeve is finished in A.

Knit 4 rounds.

Next round: Work another decrease—30 (34, 38) sts.

Do a measurement check, and if necessary, knit a few more rounds until sleeve measures 5 (5¾, 6½) inches (12.5 [14.5, 16.5] cm) from the underarms.

[Purl 1 round, knit 1 round] 3 times.

Bind (cast) off purlwise. (Do this the same way as a normal bind [cast] off, except you purl instead of knit. This just gives your bound [cast] off edge a ridged look to match the body of the sweater.)

Finishing

Block the sweater to match the schematic, and weave in the ends. If you have any gaps at the underarm, you can close them as you weave in the yarn end at the underarm.

Sew on the buttons, being careful to line them up exactly with the buttonhole position. You want the stripes to meet at the front.

simple raglan
pullover

Here's a project that's going to bring together all the skills and techniques you've learned so far. This simple, long-sleeve women's sweater features a wide neckline, raglan sleeves and a flattering silhouette. A textured panel, eye-catching but simple to knit, is worked at the center front. And with its top-down, seamless construction, this sweater requires very little finishing.

Skills Needed

Working in the round, increasing and decreasing, picking up stitches

Finished Measurements

Finished bust: 34¼ (38¾, 43, 46¾, 50¼, 54¾) inches (87 [98.5, 109.25, 118.75, 127.75, 139] cm)

Length from highest point of shoulder: 24 (25, 25½, 26¼, 26¾, 27½) inches (61 [63.5, 64.75, 66.75, 68, 69.75] cm)

This sweater is meant to wear with 1 to 3 inches (2.5 to 7.5cm) of positive ease.

Yarn

8 (9, 10, 11, 12, 14) balls medium (worsted or aran) weight yarn, 50 grams/109 yards (100m) per ball. I used Knit Picks Comfy Worsted, 75 percent cotton, 25 percent acrylic.

Gauge (Tension)

18 stitches and 24 rows = 4 inches (10cm) in stockinette (stocking) stitch, blocked, on larger needles. Take time to match your gauge (tension) because it's essential to getting the right final measurements.

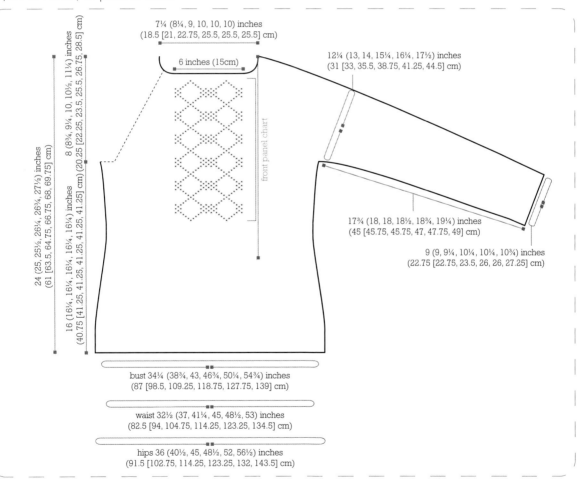

7¼ (8¼, 9, 10, 10, 10) inches (18.5 [21, 22.75, 25.5, 25.5, 25.5] cm)

6 inches (15cm)

12¼ (13, 14, 15¼, 16¼, 17½) inches (31 [33, 35.5, 38.75, 41.25, 44.5] cm)

front panel chart

8 (8¾, 9¼, 10, 10½, 11¼) inches (20.25 [22.25, 23.5, 25.5, 26.75, 28.5] cm)

24 (25, 25½, 26¼, 26¾, 27½) inches (61 [63.5, 64.75, 66.75, 68, 69.75] cm)

16 (16¼, 16¼, 16¼, 16¼, 16¼) inches (40.75 [41.25, 41.25, 41.25, 41.25, 41.25] cm)

17¾ (18, 18, 18½, 18¾, 19¼) inches (45 [45.75, 45.75, 47, 47.75, 49] cm)

9 (9, 9¼, 10¼, 10¼, 10¾) inches (22.75 [22.75, 23.5, 26, 26, 27.25] cm)

bust 34¼ (38¾, 43, 46¾, 50¼, 54¾) inches (87 [98.5, 109.25, 118.75, 127.75, 139] cm)

waist 32½ (37, 41¼, 45, 48½, 53) inches (82.5 [94, 104.75, 114.25, 123.25, 134.5] cm)

hips 36 (40½, 45, 48½, 52, 56½) inches (91.5 [102.75, 114.25, 123.25, 132, 143.5] cm)

Needles

1 set circular needles, about 19 inches (48cm) long, for the neck and upper yoke

1 set circular needles, about 24 inches (61cm) long, for the lower yoke and body

1 set of your preferred method of working in a small round

In the following sizes: U.S. 5 (3.75mm/UK 9), U.S. 7 (4.5mm/UK 7), or size needed to obtain gauge (tension)

Other Supplies

Blunt yarn needle, 6 stitch markers (2 in a contrasting color), scrap yarn for holding sleeve stitches

Construction Notes

This sweater is knit in the round from the top down. Start by working the yoke and then set aside the sleeve stitches and complete the body. Work each sleeve in the round from the underarm to the cuff.

Front Panel Chart

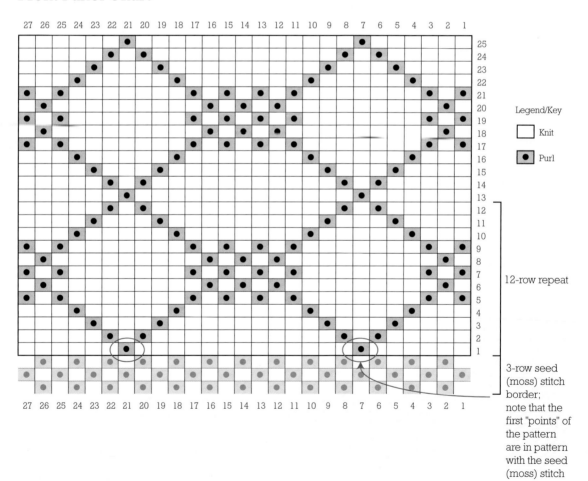

Legend/Key

☐ Knit

⊙ Purl

12-row repeat

3-row seed (moss) stitch border; note that the first "points" of the pattern are in pattern with the seed (moss) stitch

Simple Raglan Pullover

Neck

With your smaller, shorter circular needles, cast on 96 (104, 112, 124, 124, 124) sts. Being careful not to twist your cast-on, join for working in the round, and place a marker for the beginning of the round. Work 3 rounds of seed (moss) stitch as follows:

Rounds 1 and 3: *K1, p1; rep from * to end.

Round 2: *P1, k1; rep from * to end.

Yoke

Switch to your larger, shorter circular needles.

Round 1 (marker setup): Knit 15 (15, 15, 17, 17, 17) (right sleeve), place marker, k3 (5, 7, 9, 9, 9), place a contrast color marker, work 27 sts from Row 1 of chart, place other contrast marker, k3 (5, 7, 9, 9, 9), place marker, k15 (15, 15, 17, 17, 17) (left sleeve), place marker, k33 (37, 41, 45, 45, 45) to end (back). You should have 6 markers in total.

Round 2 (raglan Inc): Kfb, knit to 2 sts before marker, kfb, k1, sm, kfb, knit to front panel marker, sm, work Row 2 of chart to m, sm, knit to 2 sts before marker, kfb, k1, sm, kfb, knit to 2 sts before marker, kfb, k1, sm, kfb, knit to 2 sts before final marker, kfb, k1—8 inc'd, 17 (17, 17, 19, 19, 19) each sleeve, 35 (39, 43, 47, 47, 47) each front and back, 104 (112, 120, 132, 132, 132) total.

Round 3: Knit to front panel marker, sm, work Row 3 of chart to m, sm, knit to end.

Continue as established by these 2 rounds, maintaining front panel and increasing 8 sts every other round, 12 (11, 10, 11, 7, 3) more times—41 (39, 37, 41, 33, 25) each sleeve, 59 (61, 63, 69, 61, 53) each front and back, 200 (200, 200, 220, 188, 156) total.

- -

Why are the kfbs done at different distances from the marker? Kfb makes a little bar (earning it the nickname "bar increase") to the left of the stitch. They're worked at strategic locations for symmetry.

- -

As your stitches get crowded, switch to longer set circular needles.

Continue increasing every even-numbered round, but with a slight variation, as follows:

*

Next even-numbered round (Inc): Knit across sleeve to marker, sm, work across front, increasing as usual, sm, knit across second sleeve to marker, sm, knit across back, increasing as usual—4 inc'd, 41 (39, 37, 41, 33, 25) each sleeve, 61 (63, 65, 71, 63, 55) each front and back, 204 (204, 204, 224, 192, 160) total.

Following 2 even-numbered rounds: Work a raglan increase—16 sts, 45 (43, 41, 45, 37, 29) each sleeve, 65 (67, 69, 75, 67, 59) each front and back, 220 (220, 220, 240, 208, 176) total.

Repeat from * 1 (2, 3, 3, 5, 7) more times—20 inc'd each rep, 49 (51, 53, 57, 57, 57) each sleeve, 71 (79, 87, 93, 97, 101) each front and back, 240 (260, 280, 300, 308, 316) total.

Separate Sleeves, Work Body

Transfer right sleeve stitches to scrap yarn, removing markers on either side of sleeve. Using half-hitch method, cast on 3 (4, 5, 6, 8, 11), place a marker for new beginning of round and right side of body, cast on 3 (4, 5, 6, 8, 11). Maintaining front panel, work across front. Set aside second sleeve, and cast on second underarm same as first, placing marker for left side of body, and knit across back to end of round—154 (174, 194, 210, 226, 246) stitches. (For a visual guide, check out the Striped Baby Jacket.)

Maintaining front panel, knit 14 rounds.

Next round (side Dec): Maintaining front panel, *k1, k2tog, work to 3 sts before next marker, ssk, k1, sm; repeat from * once— 4 dec'd, 150 (170, 190, 206, 222, 242) stitches.

Continue as established for 15 more rounds, work a decrease round on 15th round—4 dec'd, 146 (166, 186, 202, 218, 238) stitches.

Continue without shaping until sweater measures 6¾ inches (17cm) from underarms. At the same time, end front panel the next time you work Row 1 of the chart. The sweater is worked entirely in stockinette (stocking) stitch after the front panel ends to the bottom edge. You can remove front panel markers.

Next round (side Inc): *Kfb, knit to 2 sts before marker, kfb, k1, sm; rep from * once— 4 inc'd, 150 (170, 190, 206, 222, 242) stitches.

Continue for 30 rounds, working increase round on 10th, 20th, and 30th rounds—16 inc'd, 162 (182, 202, 218, 234, 254) stitches.

Work without shaping until sweater measures 23½ (24½, 25, 25¾, 26¼, 27) inches (59.75 [62.25, 63.5, 65.5, 66.75, 68.5] cm) from the highest point.

Switch to smaller needles. Work 3 rounds of seed (moss) stitch. Bind (cast) off.

Sleeves

Work each one the same.

You're almost done!

Transfer sleeve stitches from scrap yarn to larger needles for knitting in a small round. Rejoin yarn. Carefully pick up and knit 3 (4, 5, 6, 8, 11) from body's underarm edge, place marker, pick up and knit 3 (4, 5, 6, 8, 11), and knit to marker.

Knit 11 (9, 7, 7, 5, 5) rounds.

Next round (Dec): K1, k2tog, knit to 3 sts before marker, ssk, k1—2 dec'd, 53 (57, 61, 67, 71, 77) stitches.

Continue, working a decrease round every 13th (11th, 9th, 9th, 7th, 7th) round 6 (8, 9, 10, 12, 14) more times—41 (41, 43, 47, 47, 49) stitches.

Continue without shaping until sleeve measures 17¼ (17½, 17½, 18, 18¼, 18¾) inches (43.75 [44.5, 44.5, 45.75, 46.25, 47.75] cm) from underarm.

Next round (Dec): K1, k2tog, knit to end of round—1 dec'd, 40 (40, 42, 46, 46, 48) stitches.

Switch to smaller needles. Work 3 rounds of seed (moss) stitch. Bind (cast) off.

Finishing

Weave in yarn ends. If any gaps remain beside the picked-up underarm stitches, you can use the yarn end to close them from the wrong side.

Block, measuring the sweater, and adjust it on your blocking surface to match the schematic measurements as closely as possible.

glossary

as established, as set   An instruction in knitting patterns that means to continue working after an interruption in the texture or shaping as previously established. For example, an established pattern might be interrupted to work a buttonhole and then continue "as set."

bar increase   *See* knit front and back (kfb).

bind (cast) off (BO)   To secure the final row of stitches and remove them from your knitting needles.

blanket stitch   A decorative sewing technique worked along the edge of fabric.

block   A finishing technique where you set the knitted piece or project with steam or water. Blocking smooths stitches and straightens edges.

blocking wire   A long, straight wire used for anchoring the edge of knitting during blocking, most often for lace.

cable   A texture that resembles knitted rope, made by crossing groups of stitches.

cable cast-on   A firm cast-on edge made by putting the tip of the needle between the first 2 stitches on the left needle, working a stitch knitwise, and placing it on the left needle. Although called *cable,* it's not related to making cables.

cable needle (cn)   A short knitting needle with a point at each end used to temporarily hold a small number of stitches while you make cables. Cable needles are often curved or bent to prevent stitches from sliding off.

cast on (CO)   To put the foundation row of stitches on the needles. This row is called the *cast-on edge.*

circular knitting   When you knit fabric in a tube by working the stitches around and around, in a spiral. (Unlike flat knitting, which is worked back and forth.)

circular needle   A needle with a point at each end and a flexible cable in the center. Circulars can be used in circular or flat knitting.

decrease (Dec)   To take away one or more stitches.

double-pointed needle (dpn)   A knitting needle with a point at each end, usually used in a set of four or five to work in the round.

dropped stitch   A stitch that has fallen off the needle and isn't secured. A column of dropped stitches is called a *ladder.*

duplicate stitch   Made by running a strand of yarn along the same path as existing knitted stitches. Duplicate stitch can be used on the wrong side to conceal yarn ends or on the right side as a decorative element.

ease   In a garment, the difference between the garment's measurements and the wearer's measurements. A garment with larger measurements has positive ease, and one with smaller measurements has negative ease.

eyelet   A single hole in knitted fabric, usually made with a yarn over.

Fair Isle   Refers to both the motifs and the technique derived from the color knitting from the Shetland Islands and Fair Isle, north of Scotland. Generally, in Fair Isle knitting, two colors of fine wool are used in each row, with the color not being used carried across the wrong side of the work. Sometimes the term is used to refer to stranded colorwork in general.

felt Felt is made by agitating animal fiber to lock the individual strands together.

finishing The final phase in a knitted project during which you secure and hide ends, join pieces, sew on buttons, and block the fabric.

flat knitting When the fabric is knitted in a flat piece by working the stitches back and forth. (Unlike circular knitting, which is worked around and around to form a tube.)

garter stitch Reversible, ridged fabric where both sides are made of alternating knit and purl rows. In flat knitting, garter stitch is worked by knitting every row. In circular knitting, garter stitch is worked by alternating knit and purl rounds.

gauge (tension) The size of a stitch, often expressed in the number of stitches and rows that fit into a 4-inch (10cm) square.

half-hitch cast-on A simple cast-on where the stitches are made by twisting the yarn into a loop and placing it on the right needle.

I-cord A narrow knitted tube made by knitting every row on a double-pointed needle without turning the work.

increase (Inc) To add one or more stitches.

intarsia A technique of working blocks of color. The yarn for each color is used only as required and isn't carried across the back as it is in stranded colorwork.

join Joining can mean either adding a new ball of yarn, turning a flat row into a tubular round, or sewing two or more pieces of knitting together.

knit (k, K) Specifically, to work the smooth side of a stitch. (The reverse side is the purl side.) Generally, to work any kind of knitted fabric.

knit 2 stitches together (k2tog) Decrease 1 stitch by putting the needle through 2 stitches and knitting them together.

knit 3 stitches together (k3tog) Decrease 2 stitches by putting the needle through 3 stitches and knitting them together.

knit front and back (kfb) Also called a bar increase; increase by 1 stitch by knitting first into the front and then into the back of the same stitch.

knitted cast-on A cast-on where a stitch is created by working the yarn through the first stitch on the left needle and placing it back on the left needle.

knitwise (kwise) As if you were going to knit, with the yarn in back and the right needle going into the front of the stitch from left to right.

lace Knitted fabric with a decorative arrangement of holes.

long tail cast-on A cast-on that uses two strands of yarn at once—a long tail and the working yarn.

marker; stitch marker (m) A small ring or safety pin–shape tool used to mark a location or stitch. A ring marker is placed on the needle; a pin-shape marker can be placed either on the needle or on a stitch.

mattress stitch A sewing method that creates a strong, thick, barely visible seam.

multiple (mult) Indicates the number of stitches or rows that are repeated in a stitch pattern.

needle gauge A measuring tool with different-size holes in it for measuring the diameter of knitting needles.

place marker (pm) Put a marker on the knitting needle.

plain knitting Knitting without texture or color patterns. Usually stockinette (stocking) or garter stitch.

purl (p, P) To work the rounded side of a stitch. (The reverse side is the knit side.)

purlwise (pwise) As if you were going to purl, with the yarn in front and the right needle going into the front of the stitch from right to left.

raglan A style of sleeve where the upper arm and shoulder are diagonally shaped from the underarm to the neck.

repeat (rep) Repeat all steps between two indicated points (often indicated by "repeat from * to end"). Also refers to a repeated section of a motif (for example, a knit 1/purl 1 ribbing has a repeat of 2 stitches).

reverse stockinette (stocking) stitch (rev st st) Stockinette (stocking) stitch fabric with the purl side used as the right side.

reversible Having no right or wrong side.

right side (RS) The side of the work that will be seen when the item is worn or used.

round (rnd) A horizontal line of stitches in circular knitting.

row A horizontal line of stitches in flat knitting.

selvedge; selvage A decorative or functional edge. For example, a functional edge can be made by knitting the first and last stitch of every row, making the row edges more visible for joining.

set-in sleeve A style of sleeve where the upper arm and shoulder are curved to fit around the shoulder and are sewn into the armhole.

slip, slip, knit together (ssk) The mirror of knit 2 together: decrease 1 stitch by slipping 2 stitches, one at a time, knitwise, and knitting them together.

slip (sl) Put your needle into the next stitch as if to purl (unless otherwise noted) and transfer it to opposite needle.

stitch (st) A loop, either on the needle or in the fabric. Stitches are the basic unit of knitting.

stitch holder A tool, often shaped like a large blunt safety pin, used to hold stitches aside to be worked later.

stockinette (stocking) stitch (st st) Smooth, knitted fabric where the right side is made of knit stitches. In flat knitting, stockinette (stocking) stitch is made by knitting all right side rows and purling all wrong side rows. In circular knitting, it's made by knitting all rounds.

straight needle A knitting needle with a point at one end and a stopper at the other.

stranded A type of colorwork where all the strands are carried across the wrong side of the work. *See also* Fair Isle.

swatch A square or rectangle of knitting used to test stitch patterns and/or measure gauge (tension).

tail A short end of yarn that's not being used (as opposed to the working yarn).

tapestry needle *See* yarn needle.

through back loop (tbl) Put the needle through the back of the stitch instead of the front.

twisted stitch A stitch that's worked through the back loop.

weave in To hide and secure the yarn ends on the wrong side of your work.

weight When referring to yarn, weight is the thickness of the yarn (rather than the weight of the ball).

working yarn   The longer end of the yarn, leading to the ball of yarn, that's being used to work the next stitch (as opposed to the yarn tail).

wrong side (WS)   The side of the work that will be totally or partially hidden when the item is worn or used.

yarn needle   Also called a *tapestry needle;* a thick, blunt needle with a large eye used for sewing with or weaving in yarn.

yarn over (yo)   A strand of yarn placed over the needle to make a new stitch.

yarn tail   The beginning or end of a ball of yarn not being used to work the next stitch (as opposed to the working yarn).

index

A

abbreviations in patterns, 114–15

acrylic yarn, 15

alpaca yarn, 13

Angora yarn, 14

as established, as set, 262

B

bamboo yarn, 15

beginner projects. See projects for practice

binding (casting) off, 42–43, 262

blanket stitch, 153, 262

blocking, 46–47
  blocking wire, 262
  defined, 262
  importance of, 175
  lace, 108–9
  steam, 146
  water (wet-blocking), 147

buttons, 158–59

C

cables. See also under stitches
  charts and symbols, 118–19
  defined, 262

4-stitch front-cross cable, 100–102
  needle, 100, 262
  overview, 100

camel yarn, 14

Cashmere yarn, 13

casting on
  cable cast-on, 37, 262
  defined, 262
  half-hitch cast-on, 26–27, 263
  knitted cast-on, 36, 263
  long tail cast-on, 38–39, 263
  slipknot, 24–25

circular knitting
  on circular needles, 80–82, 262
  defined, 262
  on double-pointed needles (dpns), 83–85, 262
  overview, 80
  round (rnd), 264
  twisted joins, 175

color knitting
  intarsia, 94–95, 263
  long floats (stranded), 93
  short floats (stranded), 91–92
  stranded (Fair Isle), 90–93, 194, 262, 264
  stripes, 88–89

Continental (left-handed) knitting, 65

cotton yarn, 14

crochet hook, 19

R

S